PRACTICAL GRAPHIC DESIGN™

Melvin G. Peterman

INSIGHT™ TECHNICAL EDUCATION

WRITTEN BY PAUL BUNCH AND MELVIN G. PETERMAN
ILLUSTRATED BY PAUL BUNCH

The reason many people are blocked from being really good artists and designers is because they don't think drawing a really good picture or designing a superior layout on paper is worth the time and effort that it actually takes. They are shackled by the delusion that if they were truly creative, then they should be able to produce superior drawings and layouts with hardly any effort at all.

CONTENTS

FORWARD

Practical Graphic Design fulfills one more step in the continuing goal to expand the Insight Technical Education brand into different career arenas. Insight Technical Education products are created to introduce technical topics and to teach, inspire, and motivate students to research possible career paths in technical fields. Further, the education received should benefit you for your lifetime, regardless of your final career choices.

Practical Graphic Design is the first of a series of books that will be written by multiple authors. The primary author of Practical Graphic Design is Paul Bunch. Paul is a homeschool father and a successful graphic designer. I think you will enjoy his candid and enjoyable teaching method.

The concept of Practical Graphic Design is simple. It is intended to be an introduction and guide to graphic design fundamentals. Graphic design is language that can exist without words. Great graphics can tell the whole story, no words required. Graphic design is used in every culture and in every human endeavor. Practical Graphic Design guides the student through this self-paced, self-taught workbook at least to a point where you will know if you are interested in further pursuit as a possible career option. You will be given the tools required to continue in more depth to the specific areas of interest.

Practical Graphic Design was written to open your eyes to the concepts and work that is required to produce brochures, websites, or other graphic works. Practical Graphic Design teaches you how to create works that clearly convey your thoughts or the thoughts of your client. Graphic works are produced to convey complex ideas quickly, grabbing and keeping the attention of the viewer until it releases them.

Graphic design is used in marketing and sales efforts, information, news, etc. Unlike traditional art, it is done in a production mode. In the graphic design field, there are deadlines, there are budgets to be met, and there are clients. Where do all the ideas come from to meet these demands? Practical Graphic Design will help you to develop the skill required to develop your own ideas quickly and professionally.

Graphic designs are still completed by hand in different media and via computer. This book may be worked through with the tools the student chooses. Whatever tools are selected to do the work, the learning will last a lifetime.

So relax, learn, and have fun!

Melvin G. Peterman
Co-author, Editor, and Publisher

INTRODUCTION

So you think you want to be a graphic designer. If so, you have to understand the priorities that impact on graphic design. Many beginning designers are so excited about designing a page layout that all they see is the graphic design process. As a result this is where they think it all starts. But don't you make this mistake. You have to realize just where in the sequence graphic design comes into play —and it's not at the beginning.

The whole process starts with a product or service that someone invents and develops and wants to sell. So the first step is NOT to design an ad. The first step is to develop a marketing strategy based on the audience and other factors. This process is usually done by people specialized in marketing. The second step is to write copy based on that marketing strategy. Again, people who write copy for a living come in here to do this job. The third step is to design logos, ads, brochures, etc. to carry out the marketing strategy and convey the copy that has been written. To do this you have to understand typography, and design principles and how they work together. This is where you, the graphic designer step in.

The fourth step is to turn the graphic design into the printed piece. It's a detail-oriented business. You have to have an attention to detail, because if just one little detail is wrong, you can waste a lot of money during the production process.

Many people think that creativity is a nebulous magical thing that some people are born with. It isn't. You can be a good graphic designer if you learn specific, tried and true techniques and principles much the same way you learn multiplication tables and rules of grammar. Of course, it helps if you have an interest in the subject, also. This book will show you some of those techniques and principles.

Basically, graphic design all revolves around Type and Graphic Objects (such as photos, illustrations, borders, etc.). The main goal is to use Type and Graphic Objects to make what you have to say easier to read and understand. Furthermore, a good layout organizes your information by creating a visual path for the viewer to follow elements in their priority (first, second, third). It attracts the eye, (grabs attention) and pulls people into your layout.

In this book we will start with the basic characteristics of type and it's categories and then move outward towards the structure of a page, design concepts and principles, how type interacts with images, and finally internet graphics.

Supplies Required

The examples you'll see in this book are mostly produced with the aid of a computer, which is the way most graphic design is done these days. Before the 90s, however, pencils, markers and pens were pretty much the norm in creating a layout for a client.

With the advent of computers it may be quicker and more efficient to produce graphic design, but an entire art of handlettering and drawing has gone by the wayside because of this technology shift. But you can still use pencils, markers and pens to create a layout if you don't have access to a computer and page layout software. All you need are:

mechanical or standard wooden pencils,
technical pens (such as Pigma Micron, ZIG Millenium)
markers (such as Flair, Sharpie)
a drawing board,
T-square,
triangle,
masking tape,
ruler,
watercolor markers (such as Tombow, Staedtler),
colored pencils (such as Prismacolor),
transfer type,
circle and oval plastic templates
tracing paper, and
layout paper.

The focus of what we are talking about is the creativity of your mind and the ability to bring all the design techniques and principles that you learn into action when you create layouts. There are many tools you can use to do this, whether they be complex or simple.

If you DO have access to a computer and page layout software, then here are some of the tools you should have to produce good layouts:

    Page layout software:
        Quark Xpress
        Adobe PageMaker
        Adobe InDesign
        MicroSoft Publisher
    Draw Software:
        Adobe Illustrator
        Macromedia Freehand
        Corel Draw
    Photo Manipulation Software
        Adobe PhotoShop

If you don't have a computer you can still do the exercises in this book and practice by means of drawing the layout on paper which is taped to your drawing board.

Pictured above is an example of a 15-minute layout first sketched in lightly with a pencil, then inked over with a black Flair marking pen, a ZIG Millenium technical pen and a Sanford Sharpie marker. The horizontal lines were drawn with the aid of a T-square and the vertical lines were drawn with the aid of a plastic triangle that sets on the T-square, thus giving you exact perpendicular lines. After the ink from the marking pens dried, I erased all the pencil lines so the layout would look cleaner.

This kind of rough layout is still used widely to sell a graphic concept to a client. The drawing of the girl doesn't have to be good and the handlettering doesn't have to be perfect. Just enough effort has been spent to convey the concept.

A more comprehensive layout can be done if you want to get a better idea of what the final ad will look like. Pictured above is a 60 minute layout. I carefully sketched everything lightly with a pencil, copying the girl from an existing photo. Then I inked over the pencil lines with the black pens and markers, using a T-square and triangle for the straight lines. I actually drew the straight horizontal guide lines in ink on some of the type because that gives the illusion that the type is more precise. I also used a plastic circle template to draw the round corners on the panel at the bottom of the ad.

Since I was using markers that are water-based, I knew that if I went over the black lines with my gray watercolor Tombow markers, they would smear the black lines. Therefore, I first went to the copy shop and made a couple of photocopies of my inked layout. Then I colored the copy with the watercolor markers.

This is an easier way to produce the layout, if you have access to a computer and all the software tools you need. It's also good to have a good library of fonts and access to some copyright-free clip art or stock photos. The ad was built in Quark Xpress, the logo was built in Adobe Illustrator and imported into Quark, and the stock photo was obtained from a stock photo and clip art CD collection.

I opened up the stock photo in PhotoShop and drew the cleansing strip over the girl's nose.

Most of the art created for this book was hand-drawn and then scanned into PhotoShop where it was value or color-corrected. Some art, such as some of the logo art was done entirely in either PhotoShop or Illustrator.

1
CHARACTERISTICS OF TYPE

Most people, uneducated in the craft of graphic arts design, approach the occupation with popular misconceptions. The first and biggest misconception is that of what it's like to be an "artist" or "creative" person. They think that an artist is just born with a mind that's structured differently from other people who get involved in normal activities like plumbing, auto mechanics, sales, or etc. Somehow, when the artist approaches the blank sheet of paper, blank canvas or blank computer screen, his eyes roll up, his lip twitches a little and he manages to open another magical dimension inside his mind where he reaches in and magically pulls out a wonderfully clever idea and puts it on the paper. No one knows how he got his clever idea and he can't really tell you. He just got the idea! And it's better than your idea.

The other people go to school and learn multiplication tables, memorize terms, learn the rules of grammar, names, dates, and other tangible things, but "artists," they always figure, go into some other state of consciousness to get their ideas rather than learning, memorizing or studying specific, tangible methods or techniques. But this isn't true.

Believe it or not, graphic art design is comprised of specific techniques, details, terms, etc. that you can study, learn, memorize and catalog just as you would do with occupations such as plumbing, auto mechanics, sales, or etc. The first of these tangible details most people already know and you will probably wonder why I'm telling you something you already know. But, hopefully, I can tell you some things you don't know about the basic characteristics of type.

Let's say that you have an article you've written and you want to design the layout for it so it looks "creative." You want to use some of those really "clever" design ideas you see professional designers use. But let's also say that you know nothing about graphic design. And you've only been given a typewriter to type out your article. As we progress through the chapters in this book, you will acquire a computer with many type fonts, and a lot of "tried and true" creative techniques, but by starting out with the very basic tool of a typewriter you can more easily focus on the first basic design elements inherent in typography.

Upper and Lower Case

Let's say you've written a research paper on the Loch Ness monster. So here's the most obvious, normal way you start laying it out:

```
The Lurking Loch Ness Monster
by Paul Bunch

The legendary Loch Ness monster does not exist in medieval legends anymore.
Instead, its large shadowy form inhabits the depths of Loch Ness along with
others of its kind. A controversy does exist, however, as to whether the mon-
ster is a mythical animal or whether it is a real flesh-and-blood creature.
To the scientists the Loch Ness monster is no laughing matter. Spurred on by
irrefutable evidence, they are hot on the tail of the mysterious creatures.

In the beginning it was hard to get scientists to come within throwing dis-
tance of the subject, but after a while, some of them consented and research
```

So there it is, straight out of the typewriter in upper and lower case. That's the first characteristic of type that, of course, everyone knows. This is the most readable way to put your words onto the paper. It looks neater than a handwritten article, but it isn't as exciting as it could be if it were planned by one of those "creative" people.

ALL CAPS

The second characteristic of type is called "All Capital Letters," or "All Caps." Here's what your type looks like in All Caps:

```
THE LURKING LOCH NESS MONSTER
BY PAUL BUNCH

THE LEGENDARY LOCH NESS MONSTER DOES NOT EXIST IN MEDIEVAL LEGENDS ANYMORE.
INSTEAD, ITS LARGE SHADOWY FORM INHABITS THE DEPTHS OF LOCH NESS ALONG WITH
OTHERS OF ITS KIND. A CONTROVERSY DOES EXIST, HOWEVER, AS TO WHETHER THE MON-
STER IS A MYTHICAL ANIMAL OR WHETHER IT IS A REAL FLESH-AND-BLOOD CREATURE.
TO THE SCIENTISTS THE LOCH NESS MONSTER IS NO LAUGHING MATTER. SPURRED ON BY
IRREFUTABLE EVIDENCE, THEY ARE HOT ON THE TAIL OF THE MYSTERIOUS CREATURES.

IN THE BEGINNING IT WAS HARD TO GET SCIENTISTS TO COME WITHIN THROWING DIS-
TANCE OF THE SUBJECT, BUT AFTER A WHILE, SOME OF THEM CONSENTED AND RESEARCH
```

When text is typed in All Caps it is more difficult to read than if it was typed in upper and lower case. The sample above looks more like a telegram or a military message. The first sample looked better than this one because it was easier on the eyes.

Usually, you want to save the use of All Caps for the title or Headline and for words in the text that require EMPHASIS. But some people type text in All Caps because they don't have to think about which letters to capitalize, thus making the process of typing go faster. Of course, if everything is capitalized, then it becomes harder to EMPHASIZE a certain word. Also another dimension of Importance is lost when you type every word in ALL CAPS because when you Capitalize only the first letter of a word, this gives it a certain degree of Importance.

Different Weights

The third characteristic of type is Weight. Type can be Light, Regular (also known as Medium), Bold, Demi Bold, Black and even Ultra Black. That's what's happening in the heading above as the letters get progressively thicker from start to finish. Before computers, it used to be that all you could do with a typewriter was make your type "bold." You didn't have several weights to choose from. Here's what happens when you make all your type bold:

THE LURKING LOCH NESS MONSTER
BY PAUL BUNCH

THE LEGENDARY LOCH NESS MONSTER DOES NOT EXIST IN MEDIEVAL LEGENDS ANYMORE. INSTEAD, ITS LARGE SHADOWY FORM INHABITS THE DEPTHS OF LOCH NESS ALONG WITH OTHERS OF ITS KIND. A CONTROVERSY DOES EXIST, HOWEVER, AS TO WHETHER THE MONSTER IS A MYTHICAL ANIMAL OR WHETHER IT IS A REAL FLESH-AND-BLOOD CREATURE. TO THE SCIENTISTS THE LOCH NESS MONSTER IS NO LAUGHING MATTER. SPURRED ON BY IRREFUTABLE EVIDENCE, THEY ARE HOT ON THE TAIL OF THE MYSTERIOUS CREATURES.

IN THE BEGINNING IT WAS HARD TO GET SCIENTISTS TO COME WITHIN THROWING DISTANCE OF THE SUBJECT, BUT AFTER A WHILE, SOME OF THEM CONSENTED AND RESEARCH

But remember what we said about the type being easier to read if it was done in Upper and Lower Case? Let's try the bolder type in Upper and Lower Case to see how it looks:

The Lurking Loch Ness Monster
by Paul Bunch

The legendary Loch Ness monster does not exist in medieval legends anymore. Instead, its large shadowy form inhabits the depths of Loch Ness along with others of its kind. A controversy does exist, however, as to whether the monster is a mythical animal or whether it is a real flesh-and-blood creature. To the scientists the Loch Ness monster is no laughing matter. Spurred on by irrefutable evidence, they are hot on the tail of the mysterious creatures.

In the beginning it was hard to get scientists to come within throwing distance of the subject, but after a while, some of them consented and research

---

It may be better than the All Caps version, but all the bold type still appears "heavy." Sometimes you can use this "heavy" effect as an interesting design technique, but if you do it page after page with a lot of text, then the reader can get tired of reading it.

Italics

The fourth characteristic of type is Italics. This is where you make all your type lean to the right. Here's what happens when you type all your type in Italics:

The Lurking Loch Ness Monster
by Paul Bunch

The legendary Loch Ness monster does not exist in medieval legends anymore. Instead, its large shadowy form inhabits the depths of Loch Ness along with others of its kind. A controversy does exist, however, as to whether the monster is a mythical animal or whether it is a real flesh-and-blood creature. To the scientists the Loch Ness monster is no laughing matter. Spurred on by irrefutable evidence, they are hot on the tail of the mysterious creatures.

In the beginning it was hard to get scientists to come within throwing distance of the subject, but after a while, some of them consented and research

This approach makes your text look a little like handwriting. This characteristic makes text look more poetic and artistic because it mimics handwriting or calligraphy, both of which preceded typography as a means of putting words on paper. Again you normally wouldn't set all your type in italics. Instead, save it for words that need emphasis or for quotations, poems or invitations.

Underlines

The fifth characteristic of type is Underlines. When you put a line underneath a word or words, this tends to draw attention to those words. Of course, just like All Caps, Weights and Italics, if you put Underlines under every word, as in the example below, then any <u>emphasis</u> is lost.

<u>The Lurking Loch Ness Monster</u>
<u>by Paul Bunch</u>

<u>The legendary Loch Ness monster does not exist in medieval legends anymore.</u>
<u>Instead, its large shadowy form inhabits the depths of Loch Ness along with</u>
<u>others of its kind. A controversy does exist, however, as to whether the mon-</u>
<u>ster is a mythical animal or whether it is a real flesh-and-blood creature.</u>
<u>To the scientists the Loch Ness monster is no laughing matter. Spurred on by</u>
<u>irrefutable evidence, they are hot on the tail of the mysterious creatures.</u>

<u>In the beginning it was hard to get scientists to come within throwing dis-</u>
<u>tance of the subject, but after a while, some of them consented and research</u>

SMALL CAPS

This is definitely a technique you could never achieve with just a typewriter. It's a way of using All Caps but making the words look like they were set in Upper and Lower Case. It has a distinctive look to it that is different from Upper and Lower Case. If you want something to look rich or refined, like it's a product of the upper class, then use this technique.

Here is what your article looks like if you set every word in Small Caps:

THE LURKING LOCH NESS MONSTER
BY PAUL BUNCH

THE LEGENDARY LOCH NESS MONSTER DOES NOT EXIST IN MEDIEVAL LEGENDS ANYMORE. INSTEAD, ITS LARGE SHADOWY FORM INHABITS THE DEPTHS OF LOCH NESS ALONG WITH OTHERS OF ITS KIND. A CONTROVERSY DOES EXIST, HOWEVER, AS TO WHETHER THE MONSTER IS A MYTHICAL ANIMAL OR WHETHER IT IS A REAL FLESH-AND-BLOOD CREATURE. TO THE SCIENTISTS THE LOCH NESS MONSTER IS NO LAUGHING MATTER. SPURRED ON BY IRREFUTABLE EVIDENCE, THEY ARE HOT ON THE TAIL OF THE MYSTERIOUS CREATURES.

IN THE BEGINNING IT WAS HARD TO GET SCIENTISTS TO COME WITHIN THROWING DISTANCE OF THE

Since you're using a variation of All Caps here, you probably wouldn't want to use Small Caps for a large expanse of text. The tried and true rule is that Upper and Lower Case is easier to read for most people.

Hopefully, in reviewing what you already know about the basic characteristics of type, you have also learned some new things. I purposely showed you illustrations that suggested what NOT to do with the basic characteristics of type. As you read further in this book, you might get some ideas as to what you CAN do using these basic characteristics. With these basic options about type in mind you might be able to do some simple things to obtain a clever graphic design before considering more complicated approaches.

Now, on the next page, look at your article and find where all the basic characteristics we've talked about are used.

THE LURKING LOCH NESS MONSTER
by Paul Bunch

The legendary Loch Ness monster does not exist in medieval legends anymore. Instead, its large shadowy form inhabits the depths of Loch Ness along with others of its kind. A controversy does exist, however, as to whether the monster is a mythical animal or whether it is a real flesh-and-blood creature. To the scientists the Loch Ness monster is no laughing matter. Spurred on by irrefutable evidence, they are hot on the tail of the mysterious creatures.

In the beginning it was hard to get scientists to come within throwing distance of the subject, but after a while, some of them consented and research started developing. First, the scientists have looked suspiciously into the legend of the Loch Ness monster. They have discovered that it originated during medieval times amidst a deluge of similar legends. Tales of monsters in deep lakes come from Iceland, Norway, Sweden, Lake Victoria in Africa, and Lake Bikal in the Soviet Union.[1] Also, the Scottish and Irish people had a habit of placing a terrible mythical monster in every lake of their country, making *"Nessie,"* the Loch Ness monster, seem even more transparent.[2]

Secondly, the scientists have analyzed reports of eye-witness sightings of Nessie. Well-known reports about sea serpents in general date back more than a thousand years to Scandanavia.[3] But Nessie was first sighted, according to written record, 1,400 years ago,[4] and she did not create too much of a rustle until 1933 when a road along the lake from Fort Augustus to Inverness was blasted out of the rock. Immediately there was a rash of sightings of the monster.[5] Since that time well over three thousand sightings have been reported.[6] At this point the scientists hesitate. If there have been well over three thousand sightings of the monster since 1933, the single creature must be quite aged by now. This idea has a strong penchant for the ancient legend of the "terrible mythical monster at the bottom of the lake."

Therefore, a logical theory has been proposed stating that <u>instead of one monster there is a herd of them inhabiting the loch; their offspring replenish the lake every generation.</u>[7] They are seen in all parts of the lake usually between dawn and nine thirty a.m.,[8] and they have even ventured out upon land! The latter happened one moonlit night as a young man was riding his motorcycle alongside the lake. Suddenly, one of the monsters bounded out of the shadows across the road ahead of him and lunged towards the lake. After the young man, in pursuit, reached the shore, the monster had vanished beneath the waters.[9]

Many sightings of this nature and a few half-convincing photographs have inspired the scientists to investigate further into this mysterious problem and prove or disprove once and for all the existence of Nessie.

LOCH NESS

The monsters' haunt, Loch Ness, is a lake twenty-four miles long and one to one and a half miles wide located in the center of upper Scotland. It could very well harbor a tribe of monsters, for they could survive by preying on the abundant marine life in the lake. Salmon run up to thirty pounds, and trout, eels, and pike weigh up to fifteen pounds. Since the water never freezes and remains at about forty-two degrees yearround at the bottom, they would enjoy a comfortable habitat. But what are the aquatic creatures doing in the lake in the first place? Before the end of the ice age, the loch was

Okay, that looks pretty good for a high school research paper; it's neat and clean and readable. But it's not exciting! Why? It's not exciting because we aren't taking advantage of many more elements and techniques of design that could be used. And we aren't using those elements and techniques NOT because we aren't "creative" people who somehow magically know how to come up with these elements and techniques, but because we haven't yet learned our "multiplication tables," "rules of grammar," or "all the parts of the engine"– so to speak – of graphic design.

In the next few chapters let's continue to add elements and techniques to our arsenal of creativity like type styles, the structure of the page and some design tools. By the time you reach the end of this book you'll be able to sort through many options in your search for the best design for your research paper, which, by then, you might consider a "magazine article" instead of a "research paper."

THE GRAPHIC DESIGN POLICE

Fighting Design Crime Wherever It Rears Its Ugly Head

On October 19, 1999 in Seattle, Washington Elmen Dufus committed a 741: *Setting a headline in Old English using All Caps*. Police were immediately called to the scene by horrified onlookers and Dufus was detained for questioning. Fortunately no one was injured and the judge ordered Dufus to only use the typeface "Helvetica" for one year and then only with Upper & Lower Case letters.

EXHIBIT A, DUFUS' HEADLINE:

𝕾𝖎𝖗 𝕷𝖆𝖓𝖈𝖊𝖑𝖔𝖙 𝕱𝖊𝖆𝖙𝖚𝖗𝖊𝖉 𝕬𝖙 𝕵𝖔𝖚𝖘𝖙 𝕿𝖔𝖐𝖓𝖎𝖌𝖍𝖙

A BETTER DESIGN SOLUTION:

𝕾𝖎𝖗 𝕷𝖆𝖓𝖈𝖊𝖑𝖔𝖙 𝕱𝖊𝖆𝖙𝖚𝖗𝖊𝖉 𝕬𝖙 𝕵𝖔𝖚𝖘𝖙 𝕿𝖔𝖐𝖓𝖎𝖌𝖍𝖙

The reason the first headline is so hard to read is because the Capitol letters of Old English have such complex forms. The Lower Case letters of Old English have simpler forms and therefore read easier. This truth is something to notice with all ornate display typefaces.

Important Things To Remember:

1. *What is the most readable way to typeset a large amount of text?*

2. *If all your words are Capitalized, then what becomes more difficult?*

3. *Why might a reader get tired of reading page after page of text?*

4. *If you emphasize all your text by underlining, what happens?*

5. *Why does Italics look more poetic and artistic?*

6. *How can you make type look as if it was set in Upper and Lower Case without doing so?*

7. *What can you make something look like by setting it in Small Caps?*

Answers on page 21

Answers

1. Upper and Lower Case is the most readable way to typeset a large amount of text.

2. If all your words are Capitalized, then it becomes harder to emphasize a certain word.

3. If you set page after page of text in bold face, then the reader can get tired of reading it.

4. If all your text is emphasized by underlines, then none of your text is emphasized, because it all looks the same.

5. Italics makes text look more poetic and artistic because it mimics handwriting or calligraphy, both of which preceded typography and are not as geometrically perfect looking.

6. Small Caps is a way of using All Caps but creating the illusion of the words being in Upper and Lower Case.

7. If you want something to look rich or refined, like it's a product of the upper class, then use small caps.

2 CATEGORIES OF TYPE

When you look through a book of typefaces, you will see hundreds of typefaces that have been designed over the years. It's overwhelming when you think about all those choices you have to make when you are coming up with a creative layout. How do know what to use? Each time you start to do a layout, are you supposed to leaf through your typeface book for half an hour before you decide on a certain typeface to use? When you show a typeface book to most non-designers, they simply run the other way and tell you to pick a "good" typeface to use in the layout. There are just too many choices! In this chapter we'll show you how to get a handle on this flood of typefaces and how to know WHEN to use them.

Headline Type and Body Type

To start with don't look at all those hundreds of INDIVIDUAL typefaces (also known as "fonts"). Instead, think of just two kinds of typefaces: Headline type and Body type.

Once young designers discover a typeface book, they usually fall in love with a lot of different fonts and those fonts usually look like these:

Alfredo PROVER Muse
Karavan WOWSER Art Deco

These are the typefaces that really stand out and are very unique. But what would happen if you tried to use as many of these fonts you were infatuated with as you could —even for the body copy of your article? You would get something eclectic, overpowering and hard to read like this:

THE LURKING LOCH NESS MONSTER
by Paul Bunch

The legendary Loch Ness monster does not exist in medieval legends anymore. Instead, its large shadowy form inhabits the depths of Loch Ness along with others of its kind. A controversy does exist, however, as to whether the monster is a mythical animal or whether it is a real flesh-and-blood creature. To the scientists the Loch Ness monster is no laughing matter. Spurred on by irrefutable evidence, they are hot on the tail of the mysterious creatures.

In the beginning it was hard to get scientists to come within throwing distance of the subject, but after a while, some of them consented and research started developing. First, the scientists have looked suspiciously into the legend of the Loch Ness monster. They have discovered that it originated during medieval times amidst a deluge of similar legends. Tales of monsters in deep lakes come from Iceland, Norway, Sweden, Lake Victoria in Africa, and Lake Bikal in the Soviet Union.1 Also, the Scottish and Irish people had a habit of placing a terrible mythical monster in every lake of their country, making "Nessie," the Loch Ness monster, seem even more transparent.2

So right from the start you have to realize that some typefaces are meant to be used for a small amount of text —like Headlines, and some typefaces are meant to be used for an extensive amount of text —like Body Copy. The typefaces that have very distinctive traits and "pop" out at you —those are the ones to use for your headlines. They create the mood or flavor for the article. The subtle, nondescript typefaces that don't call attention to themselves —those are the ones to use for the body copy. Why? Because you don't get distracted by the typefaces themselves, but instead, you read and comprehend the message of the text.

Once you understand that big difference between typefaces then you will have your first clue as to where to use typefaces.

Now let's try that again with a little more restraint. Use just one of your favorite fancy typefaces for the headline and a non-descript typeface like Times for the body:

The Lurking Loch Ness Monster

by Paul Bunch

The legendary Loch Ness monster does not exist in medieval legends anymore. Instead, its large shadowy form inhabits the depths of Loch Ness along with others of its kind. A controversy does exist, however, as to whether the monster is a mythical animal or whether it is a real flesh-and-blood creature. To the scientists the Loch Ness monster is no laughing matter. Spurred on by irrefutable evidence, they are hot on the tail of the mysterious creatures.

In the beginning it was hard to get scientists to come within throwing distance of the subject, but after a while, some of them consented and research started developing. First, the scientists have looked suspiciously into the legend of the Loch Ness monster. They have discovered that it originated during medieval times amidst a deluge of similar legends. Tales of monsters in deep lakes come from Iceland, Norway, Sweden, Lake Victoria in Africa, and Lake Bikal in the Soviet Union.[1] Also, the Scottish and Irish people had a habit of placing a terrible mythical monster in every lake of their country, making *"Nessie,"* the Loch Ness monster, seem even more transparent.[2]

Secondly, the scientists have analyzed reports of eye-witness sightings of Nessie. Well-known reports about sea serpents in general date back more than a thousand years to Scandinavia.[3] But Nessie was first sighted, according to written record, 1,400 years ago,[4] and she did not create too much of a rustle until 1933 when a road along the lake from Fort Augustus to Inverness was blasted out of the rock. Immediately there was a rash of sightings of the monster.[5] Since that time well over three thousand sightings have been reported.[6] At this point the scientists hesitate. If there have been well over three thousand sightings of the monster since 1933, the single creature must be quite aged by now. This idea has a strong penchant for the ancient legend of the "terrible mythical monster at the bottom of the lake."

Therefore, a logical theory has been proposed stating that instead of one monster there is a herd of them inhabiting the loch; their offspring replenish the lake every generation.[7] They are seen in all parts of the lake usually between dawn and nine thirty a.m.,[8] and they have even ventured out upon land! The latter happened one moonlit night as a young man was riding his motorcycle alongside the lake. Suddenly, one of the monsters bounded out of the shadows across the road ahead of him and

Next you can break typefaces down into different CATEGORIES. Typefaces have different "feels" or "flavors" which express different things. For instance, there are different fonts like Wonton or Samovar that express the feeling of foreign lands. Other fonts like Billboard or Linotext evoke a sense of history. And some fonts like Digital express advanced technology and the future.

For now we'll break the vast sea of fonts down into these categories:

Serif	Display & Headline
Sans Serif	Casual
Medieval & Calligraphy	Clip Art & Symbol
Script	

Later on you might want to break these categories down further like breaking "Display & Headline" down into sub-categories like "Western" or "Foreign Feel," etc. or even coming up with a new category called "Standards" which includes the fonts that always seem to come with your computer like Helvetica, Times, Courier, etc., but for now these 7 categories will make fonts more manageable in your mind.

Wonton

Samovar

THE OKAY CORRAL

Billboard

Sir Gawain
and the
Green Knight

Linotext

CYBERSPACE

Digital

THE GRAPHIC DESIGN POLICE
Fighting Design Crime Wherever It Rears Its Ugly Head

On May 5, 1997 in Cincinnati, Ohio Carmen Measleymeister committed a 387: *Setting a headline without kerning.* An alert police officer noticed the uneven and loose spacing between Carmen's letters and pulled her over. As it turns out Carmen had been setting headlines like this for years, thinking that if her computer did it, then it must be right. She didn't even realize that "Kerning" had to do with the close spacing between letters and that the typesetter has to do a little extra work to make typesetting look professional.

Carmen Measleymeister

EXHIBIT A, MEASELYMEISTER'S HEADLINE:

DAN WINS 1997 YO-YO CONTEST

At first glance it's really not at all obvious how unevenly spaced the letters in this headline are. But after you compare the above example with the example below, you can easily see how bad the spacing is in the first example.

Notice, for example, how much space there is between the "D" and the "A." The numeral "1" is always a character that has to be kerned closer. See how far it is away from the "9?" And there's too much space between the "7" and the "9." "Y's" and "O's" are problems also. The "O" can be moved closer to the "Y" and it can also be moved in closer to the "N." Don't forget to notice the hyphen and how it's not centered between the "O" and the "Y." And, finally, notice that every letter has been kerned closer to its neighbor for a more professional look.

Another important point to notice is that when you do a return at the end of a line of type, the spacing the computer automatically does between the lines (known as "Leading") isn't always the best choice. In the second example the second line was moved closer to the first to make the whole headline look more like a unit.

A BETTER DESIGN SOLUTION:

DAN WINS 1997 YO-YO CONTEST

Serif

The ancient Romans were among the first peoples to discover the beauty of adding "feet," cross strokes or "Serifs" to type. Instead of abruptly ending, the vertical strokes smoothly curved or transitioned into a horizontal termination. Not only did this make the letter look more pleasing, but it allowed the human eye to easily transition from one letter to the next. Examples of their typefaces can still be seen on ancient Roman monuments and buildings. To the right you can see the classic Roman letters complete with their Serifs.

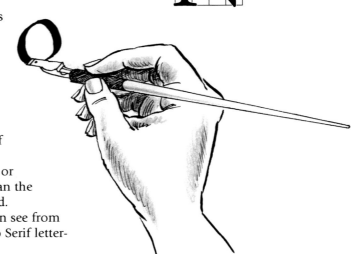

Before the printing press was invented, type faces were formed on paper by scribes who carefully formed the letters of every word with a wedge-shaped pen held at a constant angle. As the hand moved, forming the strokes of the letters, the pen angle hardly ever varied, thus creating a thin area in part of the letter and a thick area in another part of the letter. This became the basis of the classic letterforms we see today.

Over the centuries there have been many variations on Serif letterforms and most of the variations have happened in modern times. Sometimes the serif can be the same weight or thickness as each stroke of the letter or it can be thinner than the strokes of the letter. Sometimes the serifs can be exaggerated. Sometimes the horizontal strokes can be slanted. As you can see from the examples on the next page, there are many variations to Serif letterforms.

This type category is used primarily for body copy, like the text you are reading now. Over time it has proven to be the easiest style of type to read because there are no radical identifying characteristics to distract you from what you are reading. When choosing a Serif typeface you want to evoke a subtle feeling, especially if you have a great amount of text you want the reader to comprehend.

However, Serif type comes in many different weights, one of the characteristics of type we discussed in chapter 1. So the thicker weights (as shown below) can be used for headlines as well.

Clearface Clearface Bodoni Century Century Esprit Esprit Bookman Bookman Caslon Giovanni Giovanni Minister Times Minister Souvenir Friz Quadrata Cheltenham Garamond Lubalin

Clearface Bodoni **Clarendon** Century Esprit **Goudy Bookman** Galileo Boton Cheltenham Glypha **Friz Quadrata** Caslon Stone Informal Italia Galliard Kallos **Benguiat** Garamond **Korinna** University Roman **Lucida Bright** Lubalin Giovanni **Minister Tiffany** Leawood **New Century Schoolbook** Usherwood Novarese Obelisk Phaistos **Windsor** American Typewriter Palatino Times Souvenir Fenice **Vendome** Baker Signet Slimbach **Utopia** Officina Cushing Truesdell Calisto Veljovic

Medieval & Calligraphy

As we mentioned under the section on Serifs, the scribes of the Middle Ages, using their wedged-shaped pens to write by hand onto parchment, played a key role in shaping the styles of typography. At first they followed the serif letter forms of the Romans, but then they created their own interesting letter forms using thicks and thins. Unlike today's standard typefaces where every letter of the particular font is the same no matter when and where it is used, calligraphy was unique every time the calligrapher wrote it. Sometimes the penman would make the descender on a "y" flourish in one direction and another time he would make it flourish another direction.

Today the ancient calligraphic styles are still being used and every modern penman puts his own style into the ancient letter forms. Here are some examples of modern calligraphy based on ancient styles:

For as the heavens are higher than the earth, so are my ways higher than your ways, and my thoughts than your thoughts.

ISAIAH 55:9

Based on the Uncial style

This celebration of love will be on Saturday, the eighteenth of September Nineteen hundred and ninety-three at one o'clock in the afternoon

Based on the Carolingian style

February
March
April
May
June
July
August

Lord, Grant me the serenity to accept the things I cannot change, the courage to change the things I can, and the wisdom to hide the bodies of those I had to kill because they really ticked me off.

A more informal version of the Old English or Blackletter style

Another informal version of the Old English style purposely distressed to look rustic

If at first you don't succeed, skydiving is not for you.

Based on the Chancery Cursive style

Of course, not every graphic designer is a gifted calligrapher. So many of the ancient calligraphic styles have been standardized into fonts where the letter forms are always consistent whenever they appear. This still gives the reader a Medieval or European feeling when they see it, even though it might lack that uniqueness that true calligraphy evokes.

Here are some of the standard Medieval and Calligraphic styles available in fonts:

Old English Samovar Bastarda
Oxford Goudy Medieval LOMBARDIC
Paladin BlackChancery Bauble
Roman Uncial Codex Linotext
Zapf Chancery Coiled uncial Celtic
Goudy Text Poetica Chancery Aechi Plain
Sanvito UNCIO GOTHIC FALCONIS

Script

Along with the Medieval and Calligraphic style of carefully forming each letter with a wedge-shaped pen, people were also taught a way of writing where all the letter forms were connected in a seemingly unending pen stroke. This Script or handwriting style was initially done with "quills" or large feathers plucked from large birds such as geese and then dipped into bottles of ink. Someone discovered that if you split the end of the quill, then it would hold ink better and if you varied the pressure you placed on it, you could get some elegant thicks and thins to your letters.

Example of Spencerian Script, an old-fashioned style of penmanship

The really elegant and carefully written style was known as Spencerian Script. But since every person has their own unique style, many forms of handwriting developed – from elegant to unreadable chicken scratching. Nowadays, many graphic designers use hand written script to evoke a sense of free-form flair, artistry and casualness by escaping the rigid sameness of font letter forms. They do this most of the time in headlines.

There will call upon you to-night, at a quarter to eight o'clock a gentleman who desires to consult you upon a matter of the very deepest moment. Be in your chamber then at that hour, and do not take it amiss if your visitor wear a mask.

And just like the Medieval and Calligraphic styles, script styles have been standardized into type fonts where each letter always appears the same way every time it is used. Here are some examples of Script fonts:

Boulevard **Spring** *Stuyvesant*
Dorchester Isadora Nuptial Kaufmann
Brush *Kuenstler Park Avenue Aria*
Bellevue Regency **Swing** *Exponto*
Berthold Glastonbury Caflisch Fling
Zephyr AirFoil Coventry Balmoral
Chroma Freestyle Gessele

Sans Serif

The thing that sets this form of type apart from every other category of type is that the strokes of these letters are all the same thickness and they come *without* (or "sans" in French) any extra cross strokes (serifs) at the end of the main strokes. The use of Sans Serif typefaces is a relatively recent thing in the history of type. Again, this type can be excellent for Body Copy because it doesn't call attention to itself and is easy on the eyes.

Helvetica Sans Serif Bailey Sans
Avant Garde Optima Eurostile
BANK GOTHIC VAG Rounded
Univers Bauhaus Tekton Futura
Flora Benguiat Gothic Stone Sans
Charlotte Sans Myriad Gill Sans
Eras Antique Olive Humana Sans
Franklin Gothic Kabel LITHOS

And just like the Serif typefaces these Sans Serif typefaces have variations of weights:

Helvetica Sans Serif Bailey Sans
Avant Garde Optima Eurostile
VAG Rounded Univers Bauhaus
Futura Benguiat Gothic Flora
Eras Antique Olive Kabel

Display & Headline

Unlike Body Copy where subtle, low key letterforms are used so you won't get distracted from what you are reading, Display and Headline type "shouts" with every intention of distracting you from what you are reading. The reason you can still read what's being said with all this distraction is because there aren't that many words in a headline. In fact, the less words, the better.

The Headline is where you want to set the tone or evoke the feeling of the article or whatever you are trying to convey. As you look at each of the examples on these two pages, stop and think about what feeling each one evokes in your mind. The best graphic design can convey a feeling or style without being too distracting. The best graphic design can do this and still remain easy to read and easy on the eyes.

Abaddon STONECROSS Camellia
chachie BUMBAZOID DUNGEON
ARGENTUM VECTROID WEDGIE
chick STILETTO CRACKMAN
ALMONTE SNOW GYPARODY fine o mite
EAGLE GT INTOXICATED BLUES Acadian
ZEROHOUR Obliquities BARBATRICK
ASRAFEL samarkan BERNIE JUBIE
Cupola HARBINGER ECHO DECO
MachauerGlas Kashmir GREENFUZ
STARTLING Gunhead Chick GLAZKRAK
LASERIAN LADY STARLIGHT
Boomerang Black Wolf GROUND ZERO
Avatar STEELWOLF

FATSO NEWTRON Arquitectura Runic
Alfredo KICK START Columbus
Muse APRILLE AARCOVER Amos
PROVER Art Deco AMPLIO
Harrington BEFFLE STENCIL
Dolmen Russell Square Aver
Opticuento MACHINE PARAPA
CHEAP SHOT Barracon Modula Tall
Romic Bubbledot Serpentine
SHRAPNEL Revue Rubino Sans
Papyrus JAZZ POSTER WOWSER
Cooper Black EDDA CAPS Amos
Tarantella Karavan Mumbo
Carver Argos Nouveau NEULAND
Marker Felt Schmutz Clogged Wonton
Swiss Cheese NEON Viva
Whassis Frantic Metropolis
HOT SPOT Narrowband Prime RETRO BOLD
Bodoni Highlight PARIS FLASH
PAINT PEEL TONE & DEBS Nueva

Casual

Some people think that casual type styles have the most personality of all the categories. This may be because they look like they have been drawn by hand and are very informal looking. It could also be because some of the letterforms are so exaggerated and wild.

Cascade Script Matura Snippet
Exponto **Comic Sans** Choc Ruach
Tempus Sans New Berolina Pepita
Whassis Calm Contemporary Brush
ERASER Gazelle **Pixie** Dom Casual
John Handy **Reporter** Mistral **Forte**
TOONTIME Caffe Latte OGILVIE
POPTICS GADZOOX CHLORINAP
lockergnome MAILRAY STUFF
RACKHAM Bayeuse GREENFUZ
Still Time Loonar

Clip Art & Symbol

Clip Art & Symbol fonts are simply Graphic Objects that have been turned into font format. These Graphic Objects can be used as design elements for borders or "bullets" or symbols, or simply to take up space when you don't have enough text to fill the space allotted.

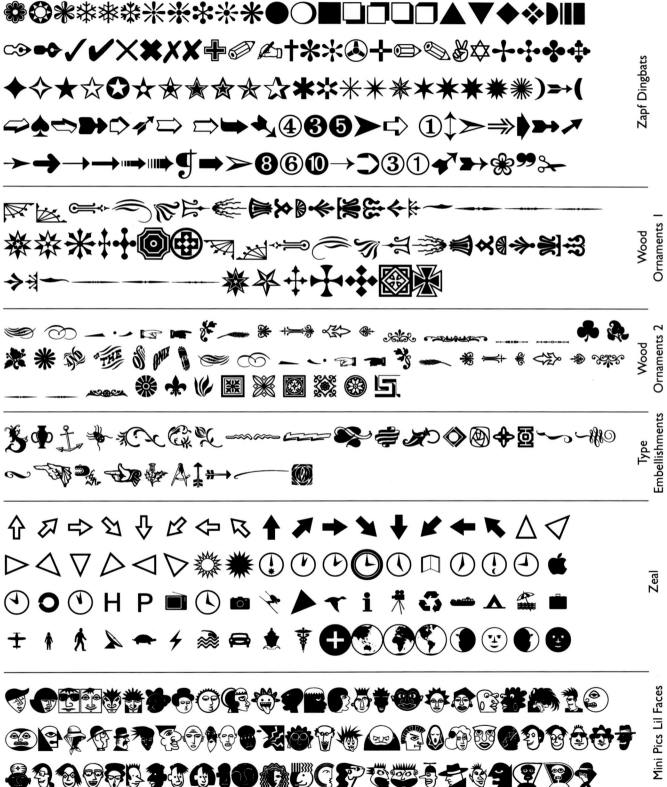

Zapf Dingbats

Wood Ornaments 1

Wood Ornaments 2

Type Embellishments

Zeal

Mini Pics Lil Faces

How to Recognize and Memorize Typefaces

There are many times in the Graphic Design business when you have several rush jobs to do at once and if you have the ability to look at a typeface and be able to know it's name in just a second, then you can get the job done that much faster. For example, a client asks you if you can use the same typeface that was used in a previous ad. In a second you identify the typeface and realize you have it on your computer, and you get the job. Or a client comes to you with a poor copy of his logo. Even if you scanned the logo in, it would be very hard to clean it up without investing a lot of time. And you don't have a lot of time. But, because you can identify the typeface used in the logo, you can recreate a clean, clear version of the logo quickly on your computer. Obviously, you can save time and get things done by memorizing many typefaces and their names.

It's fairly easy to identify the fancier typefaces:

| Retro Bold | Carver | Rosewood | Romic Bold | Wowser |

But when it comes to the more nondescript typefaces, you have to look more closely at certain parts of different letters to make a positive identification. Comparing the most outstanding letters to the letters of a standard typeface such as Times or Helvetica give you a basis for recognition. Look at the following examples and compare the parts of the letters that are circled with dotted lines:

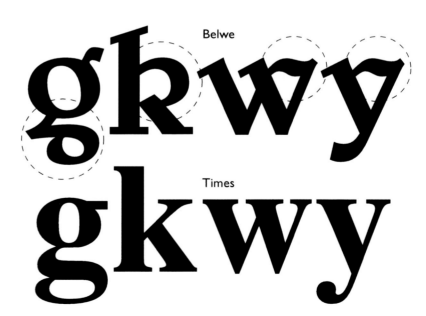

In the typeface "Belwe" the Lower Case letters give you more clues than the Upper Case letters. Notice how the circled parts of the letters compare to the more standard letterforms of "Times" directly below.

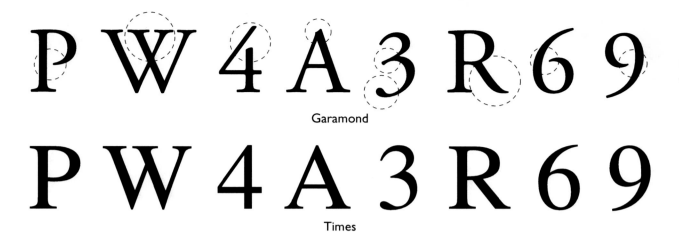

Garamond

P W 4 A 3 R 6 9

Times

The "W" is the key character in Garamond because it looks like two overlapping "V's." Also, there are several characters like "P," "4," "6," and "9" where the strokes don't quite connect. Even a small detail like the top point being nipped off of the "A" is a clue to the typeface's identity.

Benguiat   Times   Clearface   Times   Bookman   Times

Notice each of the peculiar letters in the examples above. They were picked because they are representative of the typeface. There's something different about a stroke or a serif or a shape of the entire letter as compared to the typical Times letter.

Now let's study some Sans Serif typefaces and compare their letterforms with those of the typical Helvetica letterforms:

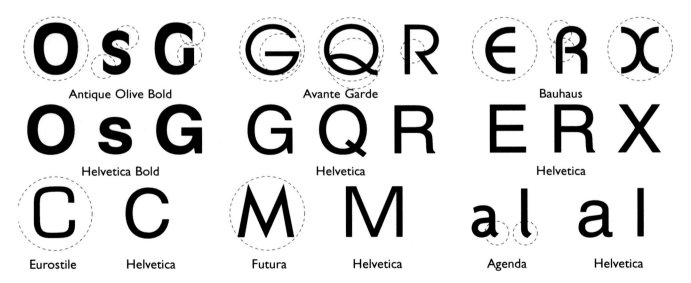

Antique Olive Bold   Avante Garde   Bauhaus

Helvetica Bold   Helvetica   Helvetica

Eurostile   Helvetica   Futura   Helvetica   Agenda   Helvetica

Notice each of the peculiar letters in the examples above. They were picked because they are representative of the typeface. There's something different about a stroke or a shape of the entire letter as compared to the typical Helvetica letter.

Design Projects

1. Make up flash cards with one to three words set in different type-faces. Try to include as many typefaces from all categories as possible. Use words that have letters which are representative of that particular typeface. (If a "y" has a real unique look, then put in the word "day" or another word with a "y" in it.) Also, try to pick typefaces for your flash cards that are popular and used a lot. On the back of each card write the correct name of the typeface. Then have a parent, brother, sister or friend hold up the flash cards for you as you identify the typefaces. The holder of the cards can tell you if you are right or wrong in your identification of the typeface by looking at the back of the card he or she is holding up.

2. Find a typeface that evokes the feeling or flavor of the following phrases and then typeset it on the computer:

   Muy Bueno! *(Mexican)*

   Omaha Beach: The D-Day We'd Like To Forget *(World War 2)*

   Death in the Cemetery *(Murder Mystery)*

   Fragmented Fairy Tales *(Cartoon)*

   Coolio kickin' it with the gang *(The Street Scene)*

   The War of the Dragons *(Fantasy Novel)*

   Jesu, Joy of Man's Desiring *(Symphony)*

   Put the money in a brown paper sack and leave it behind the statue in the train station at midnight or the girl dies. *(Ransom Note)*

Important Things To Remember:

1. *Each time you start on a creative layout, what's the best method to use to choose a typeface?*
   a. Leaf through your typeface book for half an hour looking at all the different faces.
   b. Drop everything and simply run the other way.
   c. Break the thousands of typefaces down into a few simple categories.

2. *Why should you put all typefaces in either the "Headline" category or the "Body Copy" category?*

3. *What, exactly, differentiates Headline type from Body Copy type?*

4. *Another way to choose a typeface, narrowing the choices down rapidly, is to think about a "feeling" or "flavor" you want to evoke. Can you think of some common recurring "flavors?"*

5. *What are the seven categories we give as a suggestion for grouping your typefaces?*

6. *What in the world is a Serif?*

7. *Why are there thick strokes and thin strokes in many serif typefaces?*

8. *What is "Calligraphy?"*

9. *What is "Script?"*

10. *What is "Sans Serif" type?*

11. *What sets "Display and Headline" type apart from other categories of typefaces?*

12. *What is "Casual" type?*

13. *What is "Clip Art & Symbol" type?*

14. *How do you become good at instantly recognizing typefaces?*

Answers on page 42

Answers:

1. Answer: c. Break the thousands of typefaces down into a few simple categories.

2. Some typefaces —like Headlines— are meant to be used for a small amount of text and some typefaces—like Body Copy— are meant to be used for an extensive amount of text .

3. Headline typefaces have very outstanding traits. They create the mood or flavor for the article with all their decorative details. Body Copy typefaces are subtle and nondescript that don't call attention to themselves. You don't get distracted by the typefaces themselves, but instead, you read and comprehend the message of the text.

4. Foreign lands. A sense of history. Advanced technology and the future. And there are many more that will occur to you.

5. Serif, Sans Serif, Medieval & Calligraphy, Script, Display & Headline, Casual, Clip Art & Symbol

6. Serifs are "feet," or cross strokes, that have been added to the main strokes of the letters. The vertical strokes smoothly curve or transition into a horizontal termination instead of abruptly ending. Not only does this make the letter look more pleasing, but it allows the human eye to easily transition from one letter to the next.

7. Ancient handlettering used to be scribed on paper by scribes using a wedge-shaped pen held at a constant angle. As the hand moved, forming the strokes of the letters, the pen angle hardly ever varied, thus creating a thin stroke here and a thick stroke there in the letters.

8. Wedge-shaped pens were used by the scribes of the Middle Ages to create unique, creative and fancy handlettering with thicks and thins and flourishes. The letters were different everytime the penman wrote it.

9. Handwriting where all the letter forms are connected in a seemingly unending pen stroke. This Script or handwriting style was initially done with "quills" or large feathers plucked from birds such as geese and then dipped into bottles of ink. If you split the end of the quill, then it holds ink better. Varying pressure on the quill gives you elegant thicks and thins to your letters.

10. This is type that comes *without* (or "sans" in French) any extra cross strokes (serifs) at the end of the main strokes. Also, the strokes of these letters are usually all the same thickness.

11. This kind of type is usually fancy, detailed and evokes strong feelings or "flavors" in your mind. It usually reads better when just a few words are used in the headline.

12. Type which looks like it has been drawn by hand and is very INFORMAL looking. Many times the letterforms are exaggerated and wild, which gives them a lot of personality.

13. Graphic Objects that have been turned into font format. These Graphic Objects can be used as design elements.

14. By closely studying certain parts of different outstanding letters and comparing them to the letters of a standard typeface such as Times or Helvetica, you can identify many typefaces.

THE PAGE

Some graphic designers have a fear of a blank page or sheet of paper. That's because they equate the vast expanse of absolutely nothing on the blank page with the lack of ideas in their mind. But if you understand at the outset that each blank page has an underlying invisible structure with certain page elements inherent to that page, then you can see that there is already something on the page. It's just a matter of you going on a hunt outside of your mind (thinking "outside of the box") to discover elements and ideas and choosing which of these elements and ideas you are going to bring into play as you combine them with your subject matter and text. As you hunt, you gradually bring that hidden structure of the page to the surface where everyone can see it clearly.

In this chapter we'll show you what all those elements are. Then, when you're confronted with the vast stretches of a perfectly white and blank sheet of paper, you won't panic, because you'll see all those elements hiding just under the surface, waiting for you to put them together. Plus, you and I both know that there is NOT a vast expanse of absolutely nothing between your ears.

When you look at most "blank" pages, you'll envision a grid composed of:
Margins
Columns of text
Headers
Footers
Mastheads
Headlines
Subheads
Captions
Graphic Objects
White Space

See, there's already something on the page. Now let's see what some grids and those elements look like.

The Grid

The first thing you will see just under the surface of the blank page is the "Grid" of the page. Over the years magazine and newspaper designers discovered that having an established invisible grid pattern to hang all their page elements on helps speed up layout production. Grids also contribute to a uniform appearance of a publication. And even if you are not laying out an article in a magazine, newspaper or newsletter, if you have many visual elements and pieces of text that have to come together into a pleasing layout, a grid can help organize everything.

Grids range from simple to very complex. There isn't room to show you all the different variations, so we'll show you the most well-known ones.

Remember "The Lurking Loch Ness Monster" high school research paper we started out with in Chapter 1? All we could do there was type it, using only a few limited design options. Now let's take it and create a magazine layout for it, using some grids and some other page elements.

We could format it into a common 2-column grid like this:

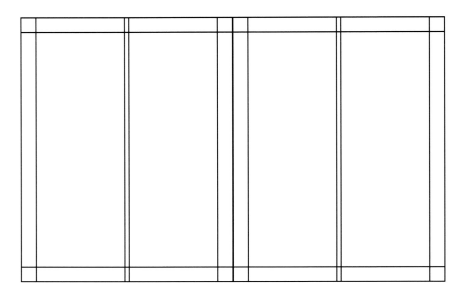

Or we could format it into the popular 3-column grid like this:

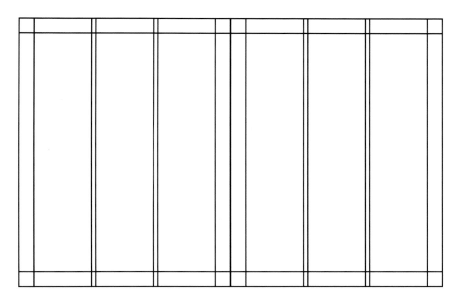

While these two grids are acceptable and work well, they usually don't employ the important page element of white space. A professional layout always manages to work in white space to enhance the feeling of openness and readability, thereby improving the sense of design. You'll find that many of your clients will not like white space. Either they will have a lot of information and a limited number of pages because of cost of printing, or they will assume that all white space exists for the sole purpose of being filled with type or graphic objects. This is where these first two layouts work well.

But on the next page let's try it again using an uneven 3-column grid that leaves the third column open for illustrations and white space:

The Lurking Loch Ness Monster

by Paul Bunch

The legendary Loch Ness monster does not exist in medieval legends anymore. Instead, its large shadowy form inhabits the depths of Loch Ness along with others of its kind. A controversy does exist, however, as to whether the monster is a mythical animal or whether it is a real flesh-and-blood creature. To the scientists the Loch Ness monster is no laughing matter. Spurred on by irrefutable evidence, they are hot on the tail of the mysterious creatures.

LEGENDS

In the beginning it was hard to get scientists to come within throwing distance of the subject, but after a while, some of them consented and research started developing. First, the scientists have looked suspiciously into the legend of the Loch Ness monster. They have discovered that it originated during medieval times amidst a deluge of similar legends. Tales of monsters in deep lakes come from Iceland, Norway, Sweden, Lake Victoria in Africa, and Lake Bikal in the Soviet Union.[1] Also, the Scottish and Irish people had a habit of placing a terrible mythical monster in every lake of their country, making "Nessie," the Loch Ness monster, seem even more transparent.[2]

Secondly, the scientists have analyzed reports of eye-witness sightings of Nessie. Well-known reports about sea serpents in general date back more than a thousand years to Scandinavia.[3] But Nessie was first sighted, according to written record, 1,400 years ago,[4] and she did not create too much of a rustle until 1933 when a road along the lake from Fort Augustus to Inverness was blasted out of the rock. Immediately there was a rash of sightings of the monster.[5] Since that time well over three thousand sightings have been reported.[6] At this point the scientists hesitate. If there have been well over three thousand sightings of the monster since 1933, the single creature must be quite aged by now. This idea has a strong penchant for the ancient legend of the "terrible mythical monster at the bottom of the lake."

Therefore, a logical theory has been proposed stating that instead of one monster there is a herd of them inhabiting the loch; their offspring replenish the lake every generation.[7] They are seen in all parts of the lake usually between dawn and nine thirty a.m.,[8] and they have even ventured out upon land! The latter happened one moonlit night as a young man was riding his motorcycle alongside the lake. Suddenly, one of the monsters bounded out of the shadows across the road ahead of him and lunged towards the lake. After the young man, in pursuit, reached the shore, the monster had vanished beneath the waters.[9]

Many sightings of this nature and a few half-convincing photographs have inspired the scientists to investigate further into this mysterious problem and prove or disprove once and for all the existence of Nessie.

LOCH NESS

The monsters' haunt, Loch Ness, is a lake twenty-four miles long and one to one and a half miles wide located in the center of upper Scotland. It could very well harbor a tribe of monsters, for they could survive by preying on the abundant marine life in the lake. Salmon run up to thirty pounds, and trout, eels, and pike weigh up to fifteen pounds. Since the water never freezes and remains at about forty-two degrees yearround at the bottom, they would enjoy a comfortable habitat. But what are the aquatic creatures doing in the lake in the first place? Before the end of the ice age the loch was an arm of the sea, — which the word "loch" means — and after the ice melted, the earth's crust rose and isolated the loch from the North Sea. Occupying the loch on a usual visit, the monsters were unaware that they were cut off from the sea.[10] But through the centuries they have learned how to live in their abode, and now man finds it very difficult to catch them.

The elusive monster is aided in staying hidden from man by the murky waters and the enormous depth of the loch. Peat and mud cloud the water to such an extent that search lights used by divers would only penetrate a few feet, making a search for Nessie, by this

Ford P. Harrison is one of the many photographers who make sightings and snap pictures of "Nessie" every year. Unfortunately, all of these photos are never very clear.

impossible.[11] The loch also has a maximum depth of 754 feet and more than half reaches down to seven hundred feet.[12] To the scientists trying to effect the capture of the monsters all of this proves to be quite a brick wall.

WHAT DOES NESSIE LOOK LIKE?

It even hides most of the monster's physical appearance. Revealing just enough form in all sightings, the monster gives rise to skepticism and suggested explanations. One explanation proposes that the monster is merely a giant eel. Eel larvae have been discovered at sea large enough to turn into eels the size of telephone poles.[13] Another explanation suggests that a giant salamander haunts the loch. Finally, there is the suggestion that the monster is a plesiosaur, an aquatic dinosaur that supposedly became extinct seventy million years ago.[14] Is this what the mystery monster really is? Listing from one to seven humps on the monster's back, most sightings might agree with the gigantic eel as its pliant coils (seven?) ripple through the waves, but what about the long neck curving out of the water in a lot of sightings?[15] An examination of the plesiosaur, Elasomasaurus, might reveal the answer. Adapted for life in the open sea, it grew to a thirty-foot length. It had a barrel-shaped body, four paddle-like limbs, a long slender neck, and a tiny head with a large mouth.[16] Supporting this idea further, a description

drawn up by Dr. Antoon Cornelius Oudemans in the latter half of the nineteenth century parallels the one just given. As he was investigating into reports of sea serpents in general, Oudemans sorted through the many reports, came up with 162 he accepted as being true, and pieced together an animal that looked like a brontosaur with flippers instead of legs (or a plesiosaur).[17]

This almost unbelievable explanation would be laughed down by a lot of people. Nevertheless, a great number of thinking people are assuming straight faces as they begin to think about Nessie seriously.

LOCH NESS RESEARCH

ORGANIZATIONS

Tim Dinsdale is one of these people. Interested in seeing the monster, Dinsdale waited six days by the loch in April of 1960; he saw nothing. Then, as he was leaving, he spotted the monster 1,300 yards out from the shore! Quickly he grabbed his sixteen millimeter movie camera and shot forty feet of the monster swimming away from him.[18] The Joint Air Reconnaissance Intelligence Center (JARIC) studied the film in the greatest detail and released a two-thousand word document concluding that Loch Ness holds an object that is probably alive. This document suddenly gave the Loch Ness monster reality and respectability.[19]

In fact, the monster had such a ring of reality that in 1962 the universities of Oxford and Cambridge sent a summertime expedition equipped with radar to the loch. But success

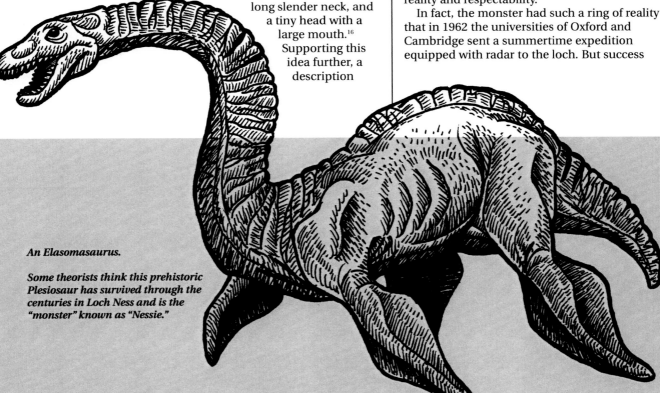

An Elasomasaurus.

Some theorists think this prehistoric Plesiosaur has survived through the centuries in Loch Ness and is the "monster" known as "Nessie."

Here's how the grid lines look in relation to the article layout. Below you can see how many of the page elements mentioned earlier were treated in this layout. Notice how even a simple rectangle of gray can be utilized as a graphic object and suggests the water the monster is swimming in.

Another eye-catching technique is to have the text of your article flow around the shape of a graphic object. In this case the type "runs around" the curved neck of "Nessie."

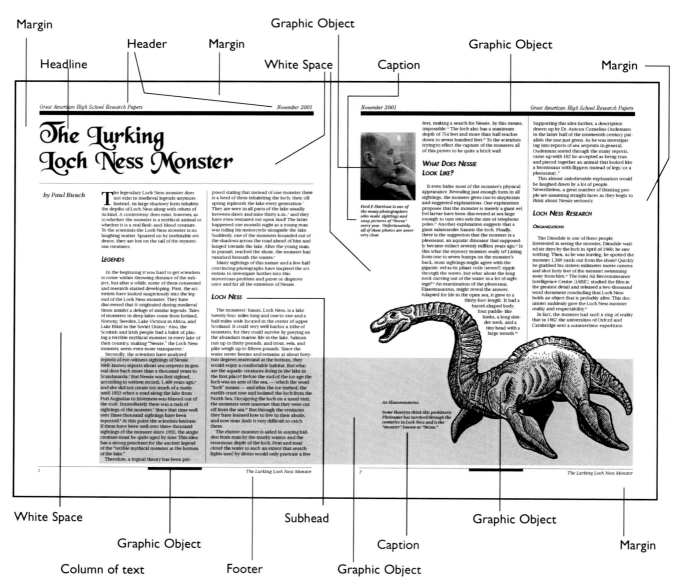

Margin · Header · Margin · Graphic Object · Graphic Object · Margin

Headline · White Space · Caption

The Lurking Loch Ness Monster

by Paul Bunch

The legendary Loch Ness monster does not exist in medieval legends anymore. Instead, its large shadowy form inhabits the depths of Loch Ness along with others of its kind. A controversy does exist, however, as to whether the monster is a mythical animal or whether it is a real flesh-and-blood creature. To the scientists the Loch Ness monster is no laughing matter. Spurred on by irrefutable evidence, they are hot on the tail of the mysterious creatures.

LEGENDS

In the beginning it was hard to get scientists to come within throwing distance of the subject, but after a while, some of them consented and research started developing. First, the scientists have looked suspiciously into the legend of the Loch Ness monster. They have discovered that it originated during medieval times amidst a deluge of similar legends. Tales of monsters in deep deep lakes come from Iceland, Norway, Sweden, Lake Victoria in Africa, and Lake Bikal in the Soviet Union. Also, the Scottish and Irish people had a habit of placing a terrible mythical monster in every lake of their country, making "Nessie," the Loch Ness monster, seem even more transparent.

Secondly, the scientists have analyzed reports of eye-witness sightings of Nessie. Well-known reports about sea serpents in general date back more than a thousand years to Scandanavia. But Nessie was first sighted, according to written record, 1,400 years ago, and she did not create too much of a rustle until 1933 when a road along the lake from Fort Augustus to Inverness was blasted out of the rock. Immediately there was a rash of sightings of the monster. Since that time well over three thousand sightings have been reported. At this point the scientists hesitate. If there have been well over three thousand sightings of the monster since 1933, the single creature must be quite aged by now. This idea has a strong penchant for the ancient legend of the "terrible mythical monster at the bottom of the lake."

Therefore, a logical theory has been proposed stating that instead of one monster there is a herd of them inhabiting the loch; their offspring replenish the lake every generation. They are seen in all parts of the lake usually between dawn and nine thirty a.m., and they have even ventured out upon land. The latter happened one moonlit night as a young man was riding his motorcycle alongside the lake. Suddenly, one of the monsters bounded out of the shadows across the road ahead of him and lunged towards the lake. After the young man, in pursuit, reached the shore, the monster had vanished beneath the waters.

Many sightings of this nature and a few half-convincing photographs have inspired the scientists to investigate further into this mysterious problem and prove or disprove once and for all the existence of Nessie.

LOCH NESS

The monsters' haunt, Loch Ness, is a lake twenty-four miles long and one to one and a half miles wide located in the center of upper Scotland. It could very well harbor a tribe of monsters, for they could survive by preying on the abundant marine life in the lake. Salmon run up to thirty pounds, and trout, eels, and pike weigh up to fifteen pounds. Since the water never freezes and remains at about forty-two degrees yearround at the bottom, they would enjoy a comfortable habitat. But what are the aquatic creatures doing in the lake in the first place? Before the end of the ice age the loch was an arm of the sea,—which the word "loch" means—and after the ice melted, the earth's crust rose and isolated the loch from North Sea. Occupying the loch on a usual visit, the monsters were unaware that they were cut off from the sea. But through the centuries they have learned how to live in their abode, and now man finds it very difficult to catch them.

The elusive monster is aided in staying hidden from man by the murky waters and the enormous depth of the loch. Peat and mud cloud the water to such an extent that search lights used by divers would only pnetrate a few feet, making a search for Nessie, by this means, impossible. The loch also has a maximum depth of 754 feet and more than half reaches down to seven hundred feet. To the scientists trying to effect the capture of the monsters all of this proves to be quite a brick wall

WHAT DOES NESSIE LOOK LIKE?

It even hides most of the monster's physical appearance. Revealing just enough form in all sightings, the monster gives rise to skepticism and suggested explanations. One explanation proposes that the monster is merely a giant eel. Eel larvae have been discovered at sea large enough to turn into eels the size of telephone poles. Another explanation suggests that a giant salamander haunts the loch. Finally, there is the suggestion that the monster is a plesiosaur, an aquatic dinosaur that supposedly became extinct seventy million years ago. Is this what the mystery monster really is? Listing from one to seven humps on the monster's back, most sightings might agree with the gigantic eel as its pliant coils (seven?) ripple through the waves, but what about the long neck curving out of the water in a lot of sightings? An examination of the plesiosaur, Elasomasaurus, might reveal the answer. Adapted for life in the open sea, it grew to a thirty-foot length. It had a barrel-shaped body, four paddle-like limbs, a long slender neck, and a tiny head with a large mouth.

Ford F. Harrison is one of the many photographers who make sightings and snap pictures of "Nessie" every year. Unfortunately, all of these photos are never very clear.

An Elasomasaurus.

Some theorists think this prehistoric Plesiosaur has survived through the centuries in Loch Ness and is the "monster" known as "Nessie."

Supporting this idea further, a description drawn up by Dr. Anton Cornelius Oudemans in the latter half of the nineteenth century parallels the one just given. As he was investigating into reports of sea serpents in general, Oudemans sorted through the many reports, came up with 162 he accepted as being true, and pieced together an animal that looked like a brontosaur with flippers instead of legs (or a plesiosaur).

This almost unbelievable explanation would be laughed down by a lot of people. Nevertheless, a great number of thinking people are assuming straight faces as they begin to think about Nessie seriously.

LOCH NESS RESEARCH

ORGANIZATIONS

Tim Dinsdale is one of these people. Interested in seeing the monster, Dinsdale waited six days for the loch in April of 1960; he saw nothing. Then, as he was leaving, he spotted the monster 1,300 yards out from the shore! Quickly he grabbed his sixteen milimeter movie camera and shot forty feet of the monster swimming away from him. The Joint Air Reconnaissance Intelligence Center (JARIC) studied the film in the greatest detail and released a two-thousand word document concluding that Loch Ness holds an object that is probably alive. This document suddenly gave the Loch Ness monster reality and respectability.

In fact, the monster had such a ring of reality that in 1962 the universities of Oxford and Cambridge sent a summertime expedition

White Space · Graphic Object · Column of text · Footer · Subhead · Graphic Object · Caption · Graphic Object · Margin

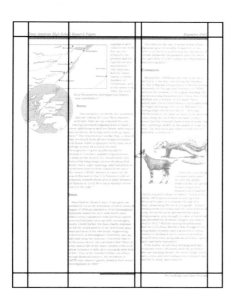

Another important thing to remember in designing pages in an article is that you should design a "Spread" of 2 pages at the same time so that they look good together. In this article about the Loch Ness monster the gray panel stretching across both pages ties the pages together. Also, the white space on one page balances the white space on the second page just as the headline on the top of the first page balances the drawing of "Nessie" on the bottom of the second page.

Below and on the next page, you can see the third and final page of the article. Even though it has to be seen by itself, it still employs the same grid and use of white space that the other two pages did and functions well on its own.

Margin

Header

Graphic Object

Graphic Object

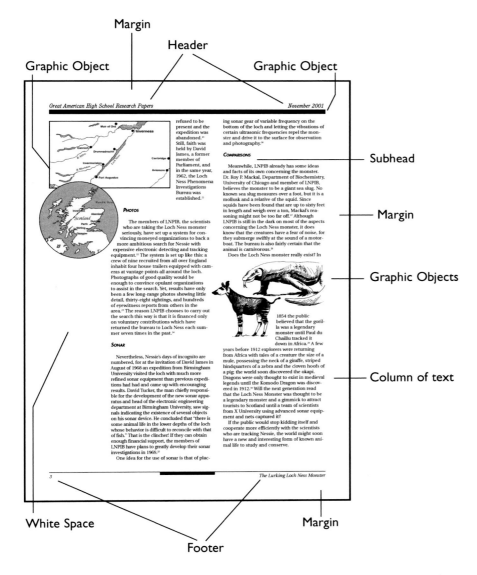

Subhead

Margin

Graphic Objects

Column of text

White Space

Margin

Footer

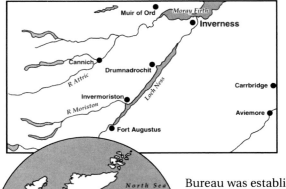

refused to be present and the expedition was abandoned.[20] Still, faith was held by David James, a former member of Parliament, and in the same year, 1962, the Loch Ness Phenomena Investigations Bureau was established.[21]

PHOTOS

The members of LNPIB, the scientists who are taking the Loch Ness monster seriously, have set up a system for convincing moneyed organizations to back a more ambitious search for Nessie with expensive electronic detecting and tracking equipment.[22] The system is set up like this: a crew of nine recruited from all over England inhabit four house trailers equipped with cameras at vantage points all around the loch. Photographs of good quality would be enough to convince opulent organizations to assist in the search. Yet, results have only been a few long-range photos showing little detail, thirty-eight sightings, and hundreds of eyewitness reports from others in the area.[23] The reason LNPIB chooses to carry out the search this way is that it is financed only on voluntary contributions which have returned the bureau to Loch Ness each summer seven times in the past.[24]

SONAR

Nevertheless, Nessie's days of incognito are numbered, for at the invitation of David James in August of 1968 an expedition from Birmingham University visited the loch with much more refined sonar equipment than previous expeditions had had and came up with encouraging results. David Tucker, the man chiefly responsible for the development of the new sonar apparatus and head of the electronic engineering department at Birmingham University, saw signals indicating the existence of several objects on his sonar device. He concluded that "there is some animal life in the lower depths of the loch whose behavior is difficult to reconcile with that of fish." That is the clincher! If they can obtain enough financial support, the members of LNPIB have plans to greatly develop their sonar investigations in 1969.[25]

One idea for the use of sonar is that of placing sonar gear of variable frequency on the bottom of the loch and letting the vibrations of certain ultrasonic frequencies repel the monster and drive it to the surface for observation and photography.[26]

COMPARISONS

Meanwhile, LNPIB already has some ideas and facts of its own concerning the monster. Dr. Roy P. Mackal, Department of Biochemistry, University of Chicago and member of LNPIB, believes the monster to be a giant sea slug. No known sea slug measures over a foot, but it is a mollusk and a relative of the squid. Since squids have been found that are up to sixty feet in length and weigh over a ton, Mackal's reasoning might not be too far off.[27] Although LNPIB is still in the dark on most of the aspects concerning the Loch Ness monster, it does know that the creatures have a fear of noise, for they submerge swiftly at the sound of a motorboat. The bureau is also fairly certain that the ani-

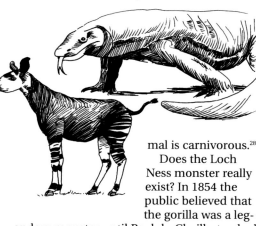

mal is carnivorous.[28] Does the Loch Ness monster really exist? In 1854 the public believed that the gorilla was a legendary monster until Paul du Chaillu tracked it down in Africa.[29] A few years before 1912 explorers were returning from Africa with tales of a creature the size of a mule, possessing the neck of a giraffe, striped hindquarters of a zebra and the cloven hoofs of a pig; the world soon discovered the okapi. Dragons were only thought to exist in medieval legends until the Komodo Dragon was discovered in 1912.[30] Will the next generation read that the Loch Ness Monster was thought to be a legendary monster and a gimmick to attract tourists to Scotland until a team of scientists from X University using advanced sonar equipment and nets captured it?

If the public would stop kidding itself and cooperate more efficiently with the scientists who are tracking Nessie, the world might soon have a new and interesting form of known animal life to study and conserve.

On March 17th, 1998 in St. Louis, Missouri Phillius Coneflower committed a 916: *Placing elements in a layout without aligning them properly.* Many people complained to the authorities about how unprofessional Coneflower's layouts looked. The complaints finally reached such a pitch that a Graphic Design Officer was sent to Coneflower's place to put a stop to the blatant alignment infractions which were disturbing the neighbors. When the officer tried to arrest Coneflower, a struggle ensued, but the officer used the Helvetica Maneuver to subdue Coneflower. He was charged with 351 counts of improper alignment and 1 count of crooked type.

Phillius T. Coneflower

What is a Double Petunia?

A petunia is a flower like a begonia. A begonia is a meat like a sausage. A sausage-and-battery is a crime. Monkeys crime trees. Tree's a crowd. A crow crowd in the morning and made a noise.

A noise is on your face between your eyes. Eyes is opposite from nays. A colt nays. You go to bed with a colt, and wake up in the morning with a case of double petunia.

EXHIBIT A:
Notice that in Phillius' little layout none of the elements seem to align with anything else. Sure, there are two columns of type side by side but the first lines of each don't perfectly line up, The headline doesn't line up horizontally with the picture or vertically with either one of the columns. Alignment of a few simple layout elements may seem like a subtle thing but it represents the beginnings of a page grid which keeps your layout from looking messy. If your simple layout is lacking even a simple grid, it won't look structured or professional.

What is a Double Petunia?

A petunia is a flower like a begonia. A begonia is a meat like a sausage. A sausage-and-battery is a crime. Monkeys crime trees. Tree's a crowd. A crow crowd in the morning and made a noise.

A noise is on your face between your eyes. Eyes is opposite from nays. A colt nays. You go to bed with a colt, and wake up in the morning with a case of double petunia.

EXHIBIT B:
Once all of Phillius' layout elements are lined up with each other the entire layout seems to become unified and organized. Vertically, notice how the left side of the picture lines up with the left side of the rule and column. And the right side of the headline lines up with the right end of the rule and right side of the second column. Also, the width of the first column is the same as that of the picture and the width of the second column is the same as that of the headline. Horizontally, the bottom of the headline lines up with the bottom of the picture. And the first lines of each column line up with each other.

Graphic Objects

Rules

Rules are simply straight vertical, horizontal or diagonal lines used between blocks of type to separate subject matter, create a simple design or take up extra space. They come in handy when there is a lack of illustration material and you need to add some sort of graphic object to make the layout look more interesting. You can achieve different looks by using different thicknesses or weights of rules.

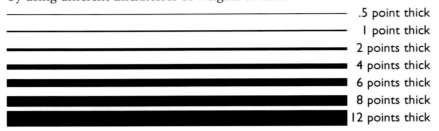

.5 point thick
1 point thick
2 points thick
4 points thick
6 points thick
8 points thick
12 points thick

Borders

Borders are also good to fall back on when you don't have any illustrations, although that's not the only reason to use them. They can range from the simple to the complex and they can also evoke a certain mood, locale, culture or historical reference.

Boxes, Panels & Shapes

Column after column of text can get pretty boring after a while. So it's good to break up that text even if you don't have any pictures or photos. One way to break up text is with Boxes, Panels & Shapes. You can put copy into boxes or panels to create what is known as "Sidebars" or small tidbits of information that might be off point to the main theme of the article but is still related somewhat. These sidebars act as pseudo-illustrations and provide added visual interest.

Shapes can also be design elements to use in layouts other than magazine articles like the page divider used in a 4-H cookbook below or the home-school graduation announcement. Besides type, pictures can also be put into different shaped boxes or panels.

Graphic Objects

Clip Art & Illustrations

As shown on this page, there are many approaches you can take to illustration. You can be really "tight" and precise with a Technical Illustration or "loose" and rough with a sketchy Line Drawing. You can add a whimsical and humorous mood to your layout by drawing a cartoon or you can render a serious, almost photographic painting or pencil drawing.

Illustrations can take the form of portraits, landscapes, still lifes, or montages. The Montage is where you combine many elements into a pleasing composition. These elements can either look "pasted" together or can softly blend to create a movie poster or book jacket look.

And if you can't draw worth beans, then there are always Clip Art CD collections you can choose illustrations from. But anyway you achieve the illustrations, there are all kinds of ways to lend variety to them.

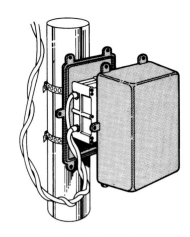

Technical illustration

Cartoon

Montage Painting

Grayscale Portrait Pencil Drawing

Sketchy line drawing

Clip Art

Photos

Clip Art and Illustrations can employ a rich diversification in style by the way the artist uses the basic elements of design. For instance, he can leave the world of reality by exaggerating lines or shading or shapes to create a unique look to his illustration. Photos, however, usually have a much different look than illustrations because they realistically depict the world around us and the style of the photographer is usually evidenced in a more subtle way by use of composition, lighting and poses or angles of view.

Sometimes it's hard to tell where Illustrations leave off and Photos begin because some artists can paint things so realistically that they look like photos and photos can be arranged in montages or retouched to look like illustrations.

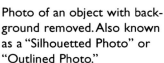

Photo of an object with background removed. Also known as a "Silhouetted Photo" or "Outlined Photo."

Cartouches and Dingbats

These mini-designs come in handy when you want to add geometric or abstract design to your layout. The example to the right shows how you can create an interaction between the typefaces and the cartouches to create a layout with flourish and panache

Another use for cartouches is to take up space between blocks of copy when you don't have enough text to fill your page.

Sometimes repeating one dingbat, like the stars below, can create a border or "line" to put between elements on a page.

Graphic Objects

Logos

There are many different approaches to logo design, which we will learn about later on. But, basically logos communicate an image and an identity of a company. If nothing else is coming to mind, you can always use the company's logo on the page as a Graphic Object.

Pull Quotes

So you're laying out or typesetting this long article and when you finish, all you see are solid columns of text. In this particular case you don't have any illustrations or photos to use in your article to make it more visually appealing, either because there is no room or there is no artwork. This is the perfect opportunity to "pull" short, interesting, shocking or thought-provoking quotes from the article and set them in larger type on the page right in the middle of the visually boring text. The idea is to draw the reader into the article because he read the shocking quote and wants to find out more.

You can either just enlarge the type and place it between two rules like the example below, or you can really dress it up or design it like the two examples to the right, which will make the quotes look like illustrations.

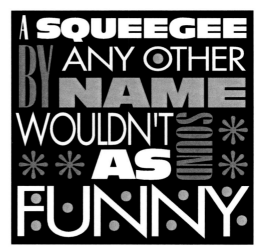

"Drawing on my fine command of language, I said nothing."

Backgrounds

Background designs are another way to add design to your page. Usually you put type and photos over the backgrounds, but you have to be careful to keep your backgrounds simple and light in value or else you won't be able to read the text.

In the sample at the right, the paisley pattern is too dark and too busy or detailed to put small type over it and still have it read easily. But when you put large, heavy Display Type over it, like the "B," then it's readable.

Small type placed over this background is hard to read.

Mastheads

Mastheads are graphic objects that are usually limited to the front page of newsletters. Once they are designed, they traditionally remain the same issue after issue so that the reading audience can form a familiarity with their identity. Their design should be strong, simple and uncluttered and usually includes the date, volume number, issue number, the address of the company, a short description about what the publication is and maybe even a slogan. Some mastheads incorporate the organization's logo or an illustration into their design as well.

Design Projects

1. Get some old magazines from the library, around the house or from some neighbors and cut out various page elements like columns of copy, headlines, photos, illustrations, pull quotes, etc. Try to get elements from different magazines to mix together – the more diverse the better. And it doesn't matter if nothing relates or makes sense. All you are trying to do in this exercise is align things and make things look pleasing. Get some graph paper or a T-square, triangle and drawing board– two ways to accurately line things up on paper. The idea is to paste all the elements onto the page and see how many ways you can align all the elements. Refer to the Graphic Design Police and other parts of this chapter for ideas on how to align things. You can align a headline to the top or bottom of a photo. You can align a column of text to the side of a photo. Remember to align both vertically and horizontally. If you had to, you could even resize or crop pictures to make a certain alignment work better.

2. If you have a computer and a page layout program, try designing your own page grid. Remember to allow for margins first. Then make 3, 4, 5 or even 6 columns. Don't forget to put a little space –like an eighth of an inch–between your columns. You can even make horizontal grid lines to hang type and graphic objects on. If you want to do this without a computer, you can tape paper down to a drawing board and draw your grid with pencil or pen and a T-square and triangle. Once you have your grid worked out, then you can start typing up some kind of a newsletter. It could be a family newsletter describing all the things you have been doing as a family and what each family member has been doing. Include photos and drawings. As you put everything together, try to keep all your page elements within the guidelines of your page grid. When you are done, not only will you have a family newsletter, but you will have learned a little bit on how to arrange and align things on a page grid. Without a computer you could have someone that has a computer or a typewriter type up your copy, being careful to make the width of your columns of type match the grid you have drawn. You can get your photos from those you developed at the local one-hour photo store or you can simply cut out photos from magazines to make your practice newsletter. When you're ready, you can paste your type and photos down on the paper, aligning them with the grid lines you drew earlier.

3. Try designing your own mastheads. Take an existing masthead and make it better, or have some fun and make up some funny ones like the examples in this chapter. Remember to include the date, volume number, issue number, address and maybe even a slogan.

Important Things To Remember:

1. Why do some designers fear a blank page?

2. The hidden structure of most page grids is composed of what 10 important elements?

3. What are the two main benefits of using invisible page grids?

4. Why does a professional layout try to utilize the element of white space?

5. What are the two big reasons some of your clients won't like white space?

6. What is the simplest form of a page grid called without really having a structured page grid?

7. List the 9 different kinds of Graphic Objects.

8. What are Sidebars?

9. What is a Montage?

10. What is a Silhouetted Photo?

11. What are Cartouches and Dingbats?

12. What is a Logo?

13. What is a Pull Quote?

14. What 3 things make for a good masthead?

Answers on page 61

Answers:

1. They equate the vast expanse of absolutely nothing on the page with the lack of ideas in their mind.

2. Margins, Columns of text, Headers, Footers, Headlines, Subheads, Captions, Graphic Objects, White Space and Mastheads.

3. Grids help speed up layout production. Grids contribute to a uniform appearance of a publication.

4. The use of White Space enhances the feeling of openness and readability.

5. They will have a lot of information and a limited number of pages. They will assume that all white space exists for the sole purpose of being filled with type or graphic objects.

6. Alignment. If you align the edges of your layout elements, then they conform or relate to each other in a structured way, which is what happens if you use a grid.

7. Rules; Borders; Boxes, Panels & Shapes; Clip Art & Illustrations; Photos; Cartouches and Dingbats; Logos; Pull Quotes; Backgrounds.

8. Boxes or Panels that contain small tidbits of extra information that are somewhat related to the main theme.

9. A Montage is where the artist combines many pictorial elements into a pleasing composition.

10. A Silhouetted Photo is a photo of an object, person, animal, etc where the background has been removed.

11. Cartouches and Dingbats are small geometric or abstract designs used as graphic objects on the page. They can be used with type to make a design more interesting or they can be repeated to make a border or they can be used to take up space between blocks of text when there's not enough text to fill the page.

12. A logo is a design that communicates the image and identity of a company.

13. A Pull Quote is a short, interesting, shocking or thought-provoking quote from an article that is set in larger type on the page and is intended to draw curious readers into reading the article because they want to find out more about what the quote is saying.

14. A Masthead design should be strong, simple and uncluttered.

DESIGN TOOLS

Now that you know how a page is structured and what the standard elements are that can go onto a page, let's take a look at the design tools you can use to fashion those elements. They are the basic elements of design: Line, Shape, Size, Space, Value, Texture, and Color. There are countless ways to use these 7 tools, so we can only show you a few in this chapter to get you started. It's a good idea for you to continually notice, as you look through magazines, books, brochures, etc., the many new ways other graphic designers are using and combining these tools to create eye-catching layouts.

Line

There is infinite variety in the way lines can be used. They start at the simplest and most basic: a straight line, which can also be called a "rule." Sometimes all you have to do to use lines is to create a horizontal rule to separate two parts of your layout. Or vertical rules can be placed between columns.

There are curved lines, dotted lines, fat lines, thin lines, jagged lines, squiggly lines. Lines can be scribbled, crosshatched, sketchy, geometric, directional, horizontal, vertical, or diagonal. You can put a line under a word to emphasize that word. You can link a caption to a part of a diagram with a line. You can define a shape with a line. You can use lines in an illustration. Also, look at the examples on these two pages to see some more advanced ways to use lines

In the business card above many lines have been used in the illustration of the graphic designer to create an interesting textured effect

In the cover design to the left I used lines to create a grid and then placed photos and type into that grid in various ways to create the design.

Sometimes you can surround type with a line that follows the letterforms to create a logotype or a headline. This technique works best on a single word.

In the poster below the words themselves make up a curving line that snakes around various picture elements on the page. This "word line" acts in a strong directional way to lead your eye around the page to the payoff down in the corner.

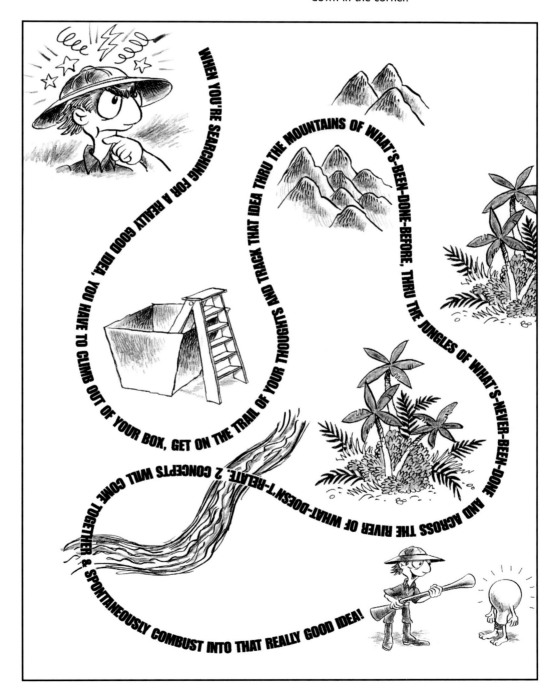

Shape

Identification of shapes is basically how we learn what everything is in the world. When someone says "heart shape" or "pear shape," we can immediately visualize what he means. On a more advanced level, when someone says "car" and then says "boat," we can immediately distinguish between two different mental pictures of these shapes. There's a basic car shape and a basic boat shape that most people understand. Shapes can be simple or complex, but they normally fall into three categories:

GEOMETRIC shapes like circles, squares, triangles, diamonds, rectangles and octagons are precise and very mathematical looking. FREEFORM shapes like silhouettes of people, animals, plants or just non-objective shapes that look like they have been drawn quickly by hand or made by accident are irregular and not precise.

There can also be a mixture of Geometric and Freeform shapes to create ABSTRACT shapes. This type of shape is usually used in logos or international symbols such as simplified figures of school children for a school crossing sign. The mix of techniques makes the Freeform shape look more structured and precise – almost geometrical.

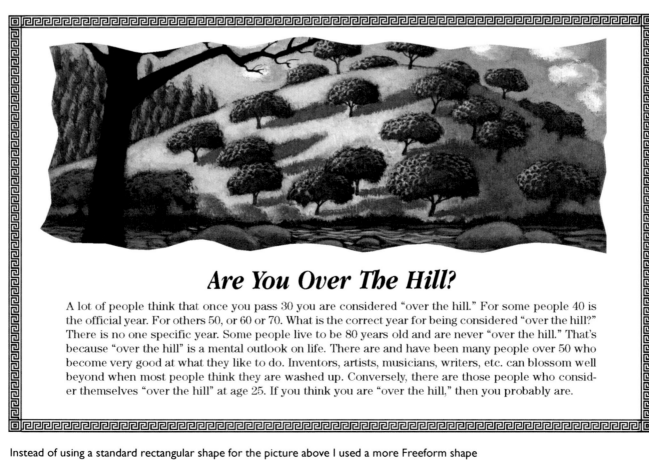

Are You Over The Hill?

A lot of people think that once you pass 30 you are considered "over the hill." For some people 40 is the official year. For others 50, or 60 or 70. What is the correct year for being considered "over the hill?" There is no one specific year. Some people live to be 80 years old and are never "over the hill." That's because "over the hill" is a mental outlook on life. There are and have been many people over 50 who become very good at what they like to do. Inventors, artists, musicians, writers, etc. can blossom well beyond when most people think they are washed up. Conversely, there are those people who consider themselves "over the hill" at age 25. If you think you are "over the hill," then you probably are.

Instead of using a standard rectangular shape for the picture above I used a more Freeform shape – sort of a rectangular shape with curvy edges. This shape contrasts nicely with the perfectly straight rectangle shape of the outer border.

In the example at the left several geometric and pseudo-geometric shapes have been utilized to create a logo. Also, notice the use of lines inside the triangle to create a pattern.

The letterforms of this type have been designed to be simple shapes and then put into other shapes as well. Here again a minimum of words and a similarity of the "BADA" letter shapes in both words contribute to the readability of the technique

Type can even be used to fill a shape as in this example. It's even better if the type you use to fill a Geometric or Freeform shape actually fits the symbology of the shape. For instance, if you fill a simple shape of a whale with a quote from Moby Dick.

It was the best of times, it was the worst of times, it was the age of wisdom, it was the age of foolishness, it was the epoch of belief, it was the epoch of incredulity, it was the season of Light, it was the season of Darkness, it was the spring of hope, it was the winter of despair, we had everything before us, we had nothing before us, we were all going direct to Heaven, we were all going direct the other way – in short, the period was so far like the present period, that some of its noisiest authorities insisted on its being received, for good or for evil, in the superlative degree of comparison only.

Size

How big or small something is in relation to other elements on the page can make all the difference between a good design and a bad one. Usually, size determines importance; the biggest thing on the page is the most important. This establishes a scale of relative importance with the progressively smaller sizes becoming less important.

You can evoke a sense of depth because larger things appear to come forward and smaller things appear to recede. If you make all your subheads the same size in a newsletter, you can convey a unified look to your design.

Extreme size of an element, such as a letter or word, can give boldness to your design, which, in turn, attracts attention. Conversely, if you make all the type on a letterhead small or understated, you give gentleness, quietness, class and taste to your design.

THE DOCTRINE OF
SALVATION

The example above is one of the most commonly-used graphic design techniques ever. Even though it is an old idea, it still works to make the first and last letters of a word larger in size than the others. Notice how you can "nest" other words in the space created above the other letters.

!THERE'S A DINOSAUR

IN OUR BACKYARD!

In this example the T-Rex looks "big" for four reasons: 1. It's the biggest element on the poster. 2. Its size is contrasted with the small pictures of the people. 3. It has been tightly cropped which psychologically makes you think it is too big for the space provided for it. 4. Also, notice the contrast in the sizes of the different words. "Dinosaur" is the biggest word, which also contributes to the "big" feeling of the T-Rex picture.

The Gallery That Has To Be Filled
123 S. Framis Circle
Spatterville, Jefferson

EUSIBIUS T. GUZULBUX
"Old Dropcloths & Spilled Paint"

July 17-31, 2001

Opening reception
July 17, 6:30 pm

Artist's Talk:
"Why I Paint Garbage"
8:00 pm

In this artist's announcement the artist's name is the largest, which makes it the most important element. The date is next in importance and then the name of the gallery. Then comes the date and time of the opening reception followed by the Artist's Talk info.

This hierarchy of size/importance creates a balance, whereas if all the type was the same size and thickness, every element would be competing with every other element for attention.

Size can be a great attention-getting device. Intentionally choose something tiny and enlarge it way beyond its natural size. In the ad below I did it with a bug but you can also use a pushpin, paper clip, penny, screw, eye or anything else that is obviously small.

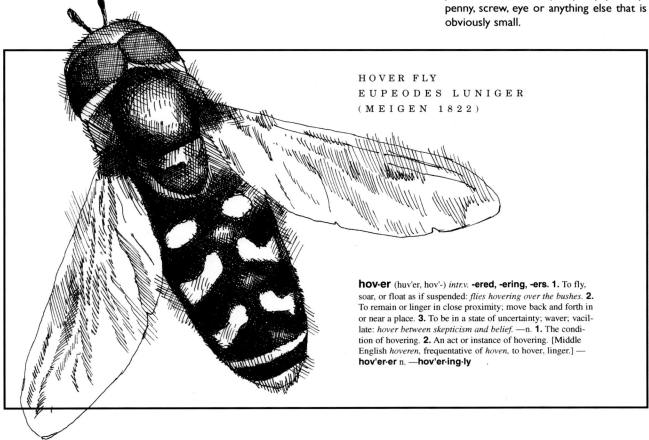

HOVER FLY
EUPEODES LUNIGER
(MEIGEN 1822)

hov·er (huv'er, hov'-) *intr.v.* **-ered, -ering, -ers. 1.** To fly, soar, or float as if suspended: *flies hovering over the bushes.* **2.** To remain or linger in close proximity; move back and forth in or near a place. **3.** To be in a state of uncertainty; waver; vacillate: *hover between skepticism and belief.* —n. **1.** The condition of hovering. **2.** An act or instance of hovering. [Middle English *hoveren,* frequentative of *hoven,* to hover, linger.] — **hov'er·er** n. —**hov'er·ing·ly** .

Space

A lot of newcomers to design aren't aware of space as a design element. But once you realize that the space around and between objects and type is just as tangible as the objects and type themselves, then you'll be just like the mathematician who discovered that "0" (zero) is just as viable a number as 1, 2, 3 or etc. The most obvious use of space is the proximity of things to each other on a page. The less space there is between elements, the more they look related.

Space can make a layout easier on the eyes because you have wide margins and you don't have everything jammed together. Of course, this means you have to limit the content of your ad, business card or whatever it is you're designing.

You can also define positive and negative shapes with space. Look at some of the other ways you can use space:

Not only can you space letters apart but you can space lines of type apart as well. In the example at right the headline was inserted between the lines, creating a rhythmic pattern and contrast with the smaller type.

In the example below the negative space between the letters was illustrated with a design rather than the letters themselves. The negative space defines the shapes of the letters which are almost invisible.

You don't always have to put letters exactly right next to each other. You can space them out for a design effect.

EVOLUTION CREATION

...The principle that the majority have a right to rule the minority,

practically resolves all government into a mere contest between

two bodies of men, as to which of them shall be masters, and

might

which of them slaves; a contest, that – however bloody – can, in

doesn't

the nature of things, never be finally closed, so long as man

always

refuses to be a slave... Majorities, as such, afford no guarantees

make

for justice. They are men of the same nature as minorities. They

right

have the same passions for fame, power, and money, as minorities;

and are liable and likely to be equally – perhaps more than equally,

because more boldly – rapacious, tyrannical and unprincipled, if

intrusted with power.

L Y S A N D E R   S P O O N E R

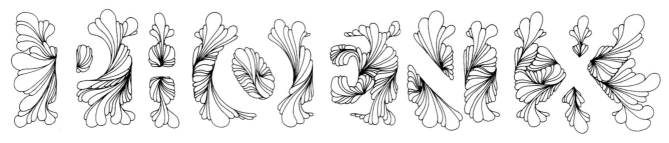

MISSION STATEMENT

There are 21 missions in California. Each mission was built by the Franciscan Fathers and funded by the Spanish monarchy as part of their quest for empire for the primary purpose of spreading Christianity. However, they also served as safe havens for travelers of untamed California early in the nineteenth century, because they were located about a day's journey apart, extending from San Diego to Sonoma, California along what was called "The Royal Road." Spain also built missions throughout Mexico and the Southwest, but the ones in California are the most well known.

Another way to call attention to something on a page is to put a lot of space around it. Notice how, because of all the white space surrounding it, you are drawn directly in to reading the "Mission Statement" above.

Value

Value has to do with a black and white scale that ranges from solid black to solid white. The steps in between are different shades of gray going from dark gray to light gray. There are usually about 10 steps in a value scale or grayscale. This grayscale is a standard by which you can measure the lightness or darkness of type or graphic objects on a page. Of course, the easiest way to relate to a grayscale is by looking at a photo or an illustration and noticing all the different values in it. Lightness and darkness also applies to type or graphic objects done in color, but is sometimes harder to grasp when working in color because you are so intent on the concept of which color to use.

WHERE WOULD $3000 EVERY WEEK TAKE YOU?

The headline above uses an alternating system of making every other word a value of gray. Because of this alternating value, you can distinguish easily between words so spacing between the words is not necessary.

Sometimes no grays are needed to have a value structure in your design, as seen in the logo to the left. Part of the type is light in value and part of it is dark in value.

In the example below a gradient of values from dark to light and light to dark is used to create a dramatic headline for a magazine article.

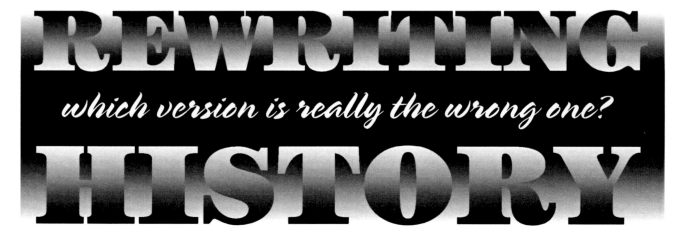

Here values of gray are used along with
black in an illustration to create a design

Texture

The basis of Texture begins with the sense of touch. Everyone is familiar with how different things feel. A Persian cat's long soft hair, a piece of rough sandpaper, a silk scarf, the surface of a weathered piece of wood, shiny chrome, the pattern of bumps on a metal toolbox in a pickup truck, steel wool, bubble wrap, etc. All these textures bring memories of touch to our minds.

But there is also a visual sense to all these textures. Because of a pattern of light and dark (values) unique to each example mentioned, we can see as well as touch the texture of each thing.

Graphic design takes that visual sense of texture and translates it to paper in various ways. Photography is the best way to give us the illusion that a background on the printed page is weathered wood, bubble wrap or any other texture. But visual textures can also be drawn or painted in illustrations.

New textures are created when artists repeat images, designs or type on paper to create backgrounds or borders. Wallpaper or wrapping paper are common uses of this technique. The rhythm of lights and darks establishes a pattern, adding another dimension besides value to shading your design.

NATIONAL INTROVERTS CROWD APPRECIATION ASSOCIATION

In the brochure cover above, the five words have been repeated all over the page in a tightly packed way, which creates a "wrapping paper" pattern of type.

The pen and ink drawing at left is rich in various hand-drawn textures. Notice how the textures also make up different values (lights and darks) for the illustration.

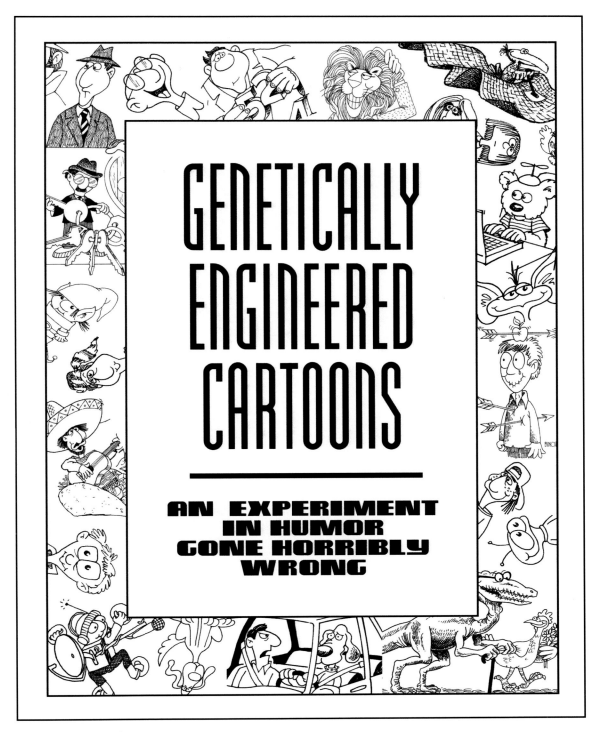

The book cover above uses an even distribution of cartoons in a "wrapping paper" technique to create a patterned border around the type.

Even the inside area of type can be textured for effect. Here, crosshatching lines combined with a smooth gradient of grays lend a sort of jungle-like, thatched-hut feel to the word.

Color

If used properly, this tool can be the most effective at attracting the viewer's eye to your design. Most of the time you'll probably be restricted to black and white and maybe one or two mechanical colors. But sometimes you'll have a client who can spend more money on printing their piece in full color.

Color takes your layout into a new dimension, giving you even more things to do to make your design attractive. The first and most obvious thing color does is draw attention to itself. By running your headline or an important word in your ad in a color, you make everyone look at it first before reading the rest of the ad. You can create moods with color: bright colors create a festive mood; pastel colors create a soft, subtle and quiet mood; dark colors create a somber mood. You can play with people's emotions by using color: combine a bright red with a bold headline about anger or violence and you convey those emotions.

You can organize your layout using color: different chapters of a book or different sections of a layout can each be assigned certain colors so you can easily distinguish between them. You can also use color to help identify things either literally or symbolically. Green can be used on an abstract design of a plant or it can be used to color a headline about "growth" or "money."

In the type below each letter has been assigned a color of the rainbow in the same sequence as the colors appear in the rainbow (Red, Orange, Yellow, Green, Blue, Indigo, Violet – or ROY G. BIV for short). I have slightly altered the exact colors, but basically the spectrum goes from the warm colors to the cool colors. The Rainbow Color technique is a tried and true design technique that adapts for all kinds of uses.

A good way to use limited color is to take either black and white photos or drawings and place a color over the entire photo or drawing. In this case the first picture has a yellow over it, the second one has a green over it and the last one has a blue over it. Sometimes this is a good way to bring black and white pictures to life when you don't have access to full color pictures.

The example to the right uses type as bands of color. At first glance you think there are four colors, Red, gray, white and black. But, actually, this is only a 2-color design: Red and black. The gray is only a halftone screen of black and the white type is only the white paper showing where no ink was printed! If I had wanted to, I could have also screened the red back to produce a pink, giving the illusion of a 5th color. This shows how you can "stretch" your color palette when you are limited to a 2-color job.

TRUTH
COMES OUT OF
ERROR
MORE EASILY THAN OUT OF
CONFUSION

Horizontal or vertical bands of solid color are good to use because they create a pattern which can be used effectively as a background against which you can display black and white line art, such as the root beer floats and hamburger shown above. The contrast of full color and no color is striking.

Sometimes you don't have to depict subjects in accurate, life-like color. If you are going for the pure design of Freeform shapes of color on a page, then you can make the outlines and shadows of your subject any color you want, with the only rhyme or reason being how each color shape looks against the other. This technique is a very lively one and adds excite-ment to your layout.

When you are talking about color, you have to realize that color is like language. Just as there are different languages in the world, there are different color spaces and color definitions. Let's say you take a trip to France. While in France, you would have to converse in the French language to be understood by most of the people. If you travel to another country –let's say China– then you have to converse in Chinese to be understood.

The same analogy can be applied to color. If you paint a picture using oil paints or acrylic paints, then you have to use the structure of color for painting – the basic color wheel, mixing the primary colors to make secondary colors and mixing all the colors in between to make intermediate colors, mixing in additions of white to make things lighter and additions of black to make things darker. While painting a picture you are in the country of "Painting," so you talk in that country's language of color.

But if you want to design a brochure that will be printed in color on a printing press, then you have to use the structure of color for printing – either process color or mechanical color. Process color is composed of four colors: Cyan, Magenta, Yellow, and Black (CMYK). These inks are like paint but you don't mix them together on a palette with a paintbrush to achieve different colors like you do with oil paints or acrylic paints. Instead you employ halftone screens and a printing press. The halftone screens are composed of tiny dots which, depending on their size and proximity to each other, determine how light or dark a color will be. The degree of lightness or darkness is referred to as a percent. So, by mixing varying halftone percentages of Cyan, Magenta, Yellow, and Black you can achieve every color in the rainbow without using a paint brush. You are now in the country of "Printing," so you have to use a different language to get things to work than you would if you were in the country of "Painting."

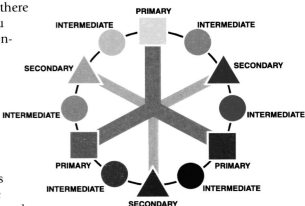

The diagram above shows the color wheel for painting. Even though printing uses a different technical process to achieve color mixing, you can still figure out what colors look good together for a print design based on the painting color wheel. You just have to translate your color choices into the CMYK environment. Below are two ways to find colors that look good together.

Below is the diagram showing two analogous color selections on the painting color wheel. Analogous colors are colors that lie right next to each other on the wheel. Analogous color schemes can be any arrangement of colors from two to five or more. And, remember, there can be light or dark values of those analogous colors combined in designs like the non-objective, geometrical designs shown.

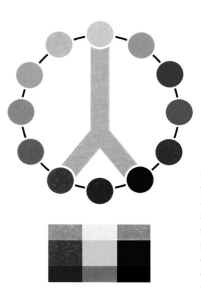

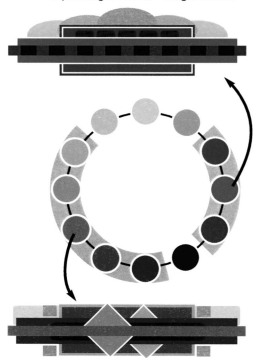

Complementary colors are those that are directly opposite each other on the color wheel. The diagram to the left shows a color scheme using split complementary colors. You can start with any color and combine it with its complementary or its split complementary colors.

Most people in the graphic design business refer to this color structure or color "language" as "CMYK." You would think it should be "CMYB," because, after all, "Black" starts with a B, but most people come from the land of "Painting" where B stands for "Blue," and "Black" is not on the color wheel in the country of "Painting" as it is in the country of "Printing." Since Cyan looks like a blue, there would be confusion, because there is only one primary blue in this color structure and it's called "Cyan." Therefore, people in the country of "Printing" take the last letter of "Black" (K) and use it instead.

You can also use mechanical color while in the country of "Printing." There are different companies that pre-mix Cyan, Magenta, Yellow and Black and give them special numbers or names. One of the most well known companies is PANTONE and they have a color structure or "language" known as the Pantone Matching System (PMS). Usually PMS colors or other mechanical colors are used in a limited way when you only want Black and one or two other colors.

Now, if you want to design a website, you will be traveling to yet another country – that of "Computer Monitors," and you will have to learn yet another color language: RGB. This color structure is based on the three primary colors of Red, Green and Blue and instead of being squeezed out of a tube onto a palette or mixed by halftone screens on a printing press, they are composed of light being mixed and emitted from within your computer monitor.

There are numerous ways to discover what colors go well together in a design or a painting. You have seen the Analogous color schemes and the Complementary and Split Complementary color schemes shown on the previous page.

Another general principle to remember is to limit your color palette. Some of the most popular paintings have been done with just 2 or 3 colors. They tend to be almost monochromatic (looking like they only use different values of one color).

In print design you can see an example of this subtle use of color below where many black and white photos have been slightly tinted with purple, yellow, red and blue green. Your designs will look more professional if you know how to use subtle color.

The original photo

The original photo translated into halftone dots and color separations in order to create the mixture of full color.

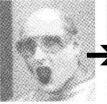

Cyan

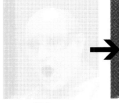

Magenta

Magenta plus Cyan

Yellow

Yellow plus Magenta plus Cyan

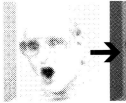

Black

Black plus Yellow plus Magenta plus Cyan

The halftone dots in this example have been exaggerated in size to show how the process works. Most advanced printing uses really tiny halftone dots practically undiscernable by the human eye. This creates a smoother, cleaner look to the photo.

The Practical Side of the Design Tools

It's one thing to know about the really cool stuff you can do with the basic elements of design, but it's another thing to make that stuff happen in the real world. You'll always have to work within the limitations of what your client likes and his limited budget. Sometimes your client will let you do a really artistic design. Other times your client will force you to do something you think is dull and boring, but he will love it. The technology used in your job will also limit you. For instance, if you run a job on a photocopier, you might not be able to achieve what you could on a high-end printing press. So, you'll have to get used to working within limits. Here are a few problems you might run up against when using some of the design tools and how to work around them:

LINE Some people gifted at drawing with pen & ink produce an original that looks absolutely fabulous when it's hanging on a gallery wall, but when reproduced, the intricate and fine lines disappear because it's greatly reduced. The answer is to begin the line drawing knowing where it's going to be reproduced and how big. Then you can plan the width of your lines so when they are reduced you can still see them.

SIZE & SPACE You'll probably encounter people untrained in graphic art who will want to make everything in an ad stand out. They'll direct you to make all of the type bold and big and underline everything! Plus, since there is some white space left, why not include another slogan or two, or maybe The Lord's Prayer? They think white space has to be filled with type and graphic objects. Try to educate them that really good ads limit their theme to one thing, resulting in less content and more white space.

VALUE Even though there are about 10 steps on a grayscale, there are limits to printing technology where you might have to limit your steps to 20, 30 and 50% gray. Grays are produced by printing Black halftone dots of different sizes. In offset printing there are problems maintaining the open spaces between those dots, especially with the darker tones from 60-90%, because the dots are so big and the spaces between the dots are so tiny. So the dots can clog up. This is known as "dot gain." It's easier to keep the spaces between the dots open in the lighter values of gray such as 20, 30 and 50%. In fact, you can suggest a 70 or 80% gray by using a 50% gray and the 30% can represent the 50% gray. On some photocopiers and presses 10% gray is so light that it won't even show up. So it's more practical to have the 20% represent the 10% gray.

COLOR A very important thing to master with color is how to trap it for printing. When two areas of color touch each other, their edges have to slightly overlap (overprint) to create the illusion that they perfectly align (register) with each other. If their edges don't slightly overlap, then, because of the variation in the movement of each piece of paper through the press, there will be a tiny white gap between one area of color and another on some of the printed pieces. You don't have to worry about trapping when printing photos, but when you create type or graphic objects with various colors that touch each other, you have to trap the colors so there are no white gaps. Vector-based computer software (draw programs that put little handles on graphic shapes) allow you to not only Fill a shape with color, but also to Stroke the perimeter of that shape with color. You can then control whether you want to overprint (overlap) the Stroke, which allows adjacent colors to "trap" together.

A grayscale consisting of halftone screens which can easily plug up in the darker values.

20%

30%

50%

A. One-to-One registration. Every once in a while this aligns.

B. Misalignment of One-to-One registration during printing process causes white gaps.

C. Correct trapping: the light colored star is larger than the white area underneath it because it has an overprinting stroke added to it.

A.

B.

C.

THE GRAPHIC DESIGN POLICE

Fighting Design Crime Wherever It Rears Its Ugly Head

On August 23, 1993 in Biloxi, Mississippi Laslo Norfnoid committed a 524: *Improper use of Size & Space in an Ad.* An innocent bystander heard a woman's scream coming from the park and alerted 10 police officers who had just bought ice cream cones and were eating them in a small car driving by the crime scene. Norfnoid was apprehended and restrained before he could put his autobiography and The Lord's Prayer into the ad. The judge put Norfnoid on 6 month's probation, limiting the number of elements in his future ads to ONE.

Laslo Norfnoid

EXHIBIT A, NORFNOID'S AD:

Notice how Laslo wanted to make everything stand out by either making the type bold or underlining it. He tries to say so many different things in the ad that it all runs together and gets lost. He's got 3 slogans, 8 phone numbers, a listing of all the brands he carries, wording that tells how great Widget Wonderland is, and he even has the Christian fish symbol and a verse of scripture to make himself look even better. Everything is about the same size and there is practically no white space left which makes the ad difficult to view.

EXHIBIT B, A REDESIGNED AD THAT'S MORE EYE-CATCHING:

In the cleaned-up version of the ad the content of the ad has been limited to one theme. The ad focuses only on the fact that Widget Wonderland has widgets for all occasions. There's a bold and simple headline, then you see an interesting widget illustration, which leads you down to the name of the store. Then you finish out the ad with only one slogan, 2 phone numbers and some addresses. The extra white space works to balance the elements and the ad is a lot easier on the eyes because of it.

Design Projects

1. Create your own grayscale like the one on page 80. Make each square an inch wide. Instead of using a computer, paint, or pencil, use a series of technical pens and the shading technique known as "STIP-PLE" where your shading is composed of nothing but dots. You can approach it a couple of ways: stipple using just one technical pen where all the dots are the same size. The closer you put the dots together, the more dots there are in your little square and the darker your value becomes. The other way to approach it is to have about 3 or 4 different sizes of nibs on your technical pens and use the fine tips for the lighter shades of your Grayscale, the medium tips for the middle tones and the heavy tips for the dark tones of your Grayscale. The big dots are easier for the dark values because you don't need as many as you would if you used the small dots to do the dark values. Stipple, pointillism or pontilism looks best if you have a lot of patience and lay your dots down carefully and slowly.

   This exercise will help you get a feel for how dot shading can approximate the values of paint, pencil or some other continuous tone medium. Of course, Halftone Screens created by the computer in graphic design are much more precise and technical, but you can understand better what's going on with them if you do this exercise.

2. Review all the examples in this chapter and pick one or more to do yourself. For instance, if you liked the border made up of cartoons in the section on Texture, make your own border composed of your own cartoons or line drawings. You could even make copies of little line drawings or cartoons you see in magazines and paste them all together into a border or scan them into a computer and work with them there. The idea is to use my examples as starting points and adapt the concepts to your art or your themes. Actually producing something based on these techniques will help you remember the techniques later on when you are trying to come up with some ideas for a real job you get from a client.

Important Things To Remember:

1. The simplest and most basic Lines are called

2. List the 4 different ways Lines are used in the examples shown on pages 64 and 65.

3. What are the 3 types of Shapes?

4. List the different ways Shapes are used in the examples shown on pages 66 and 67.

5. What does the Size of something determine in a layout?

6. Explain how Size is used in the 4 examples shown on pages 68 and 69.

7. The less space there is between elements on a page, the more they look_____.

8. True or False: If you end up with White Space in your layout, it has to be filled with either type or a graphic object for your design to look good.

9. How is Space used in the examples on pages 70 and 71?

10. How many steps are usually on a grayscale?

11. How is Value used in the 4 examples on page 72 and 73?

12. We sense texture with what 2 senses?

13. How is Texture used in the examples on pages 74 and 75?

14. The first and most obvious thing color does is _____

15. How is color used in the examples on pages 76 and 77?

16. What 2 limitations can you always expect when designing things in the real world?

17. What pitfall should you avoid when working with Line?

18. When it comes to Size and Space, what do really good ads do that makes them good?

19. Why should a grayscale be limited when printing on an offset press?

20. In printing when 2 areas of color touch each other and their edges slightly overlap, this is called _____.

Answers on page 84

Answers:

1. Rules

2. Business Card: Lines were used in the illustration to create Texture. Cover: Lines were used to create a grid. Logotype or Headline: Lines were used to surround type, following the shape of the letterforms. Poster: Words were used to create a curving line.

3. Geometric (square, circle, triangle, etc.), Freeform (hand drawn or accidental looking), Abstract (combination of Geometric and Freeform).

4. Ad: A Freeform Shape was used for the picture. Logo: Geometric and Abstract Shapes were used to create the logo. Logotype or Headline: The letterforms are simplified Abstract Shapes which have been placed inside Geometric Shapes. Circle of Type: Type is used to fill a Geometric Shape.

5. Importance and/or Depth.

6. Title: The first and last letter of a word are made larger than the rest of the letters. Dinosaur Poster: A. The T-Rex is the largest element in the design. B. The T-Rex picture is contrasted in size with the small pictures of the people, making the T-Rex appear even larger. C. The T-Rex has been tightly cropped, making you think it's too big for the space provided for it. D. The word "Dinosaur" is the biggest word, which also contributes to the large feeling of the T-Rex. Artist's Announcement: A hierarchy of importance has been established by making each type element a different size and weight. This creates a balance where the different elements are not competing with each other. The Fly Ad: Something obviously tiny has been enlarged beyond its normal size to attract attention.

7. Related.

8. False: White space is just as viable an element as any other type element or graphic object. It can help make your layout easy on the eyes and can draw attention to things.

9. Evolution or Creation Headline: The letters in the headline have been spaced out. Lysander Spooner Poster: The lines of type have been spaced out and even the lines of the headline have been spaced out. Phoenix Lettering: The negative space between the letters are the graphic objects and the letters are the new negative spaces between those graphic objects. Mission Statement: The white space around the type has been exaggerated to call more attention to what's being said.

10. There are usually ten steps on a grayscale.

11. Headline: Black and a value of gray are alternated every other word in a sentence. Logo: No grays are used in this example, but there still is a value scale of Black and White. Rewriting History Headline: Values are used in smooth gradients inside and behind the letters. Tree Illustration: Flat grays and Black and White are used in an illustration.

12. We sense Texture with Touch and Sight.

13. Brochure cover: Type has been repeated all over the cover to look like "wrapping paper." Pen & Ink Drawing: The drawing has been shaded with many different, patterned lines to create the gray values. Book cover: The border uses an even distribution of cartoons to produce a "wrapping paper" technique. Headline: The inside of the letters has been given patterned shading.

14. Draw attention to itself.

15. Headline: A different color of the rainbow is used for each letter in a headline. The colors of the rainbow are used in order, going from warm colors to cool colors. Pictures of 3 Guys: Light colors have been laid over black and white illustrations to add more life to them. Headline: Lines of type are used like bands of color and a 2-color job is made to look like a 4 or 5-color job by using screened tints of the 2 colors. Drinks and a Hamburger: Horizontal bands of color provide an interesting contrasting, patterned background for black and white line art. Illustration: Freeform shapes of bright colors are used to shade a picture of an animal. The colors are intentionally not like you would normally see in a photo.

16. Limitations: A. What your client likes. B. Your client's limited budget.

17. Pitfall to avoid: Making your lines so fine that when you reduce your picture for reproduction, the lines drop out (disappear).

18. They limit their theme to one thing, resulting in less content and more white space.

19. It's hard to keep the halftone dots in the darker values of gray from clogging up. The lighter tones are easier to control.

20. Trapping.

LOGO DESIGN

Logos are basically **communications** of ideas or images. It's interesting to note that the word "logo" originates from the ancient Greek language. The Greek word "logos" (pronounced low-gaws) was translated into English as "word" in the King James Bible. It's true original meaning is **communication**. So in the New Testament when it says "And the Word (logos) was made flesh, and dwelt among us,..." it is actually saying that the **communication** was made flesh and dwelt among us. Jesus was functioning as a symbol or representative of His Father by communicating God's Word to His followers. It becomes obvious, then, that there are many ways to communicate: words can communicate; people (in this case, Jesus) can communicate; and even pictures (graphic symbols) can communicate.

People who want to sell products design graphic symbols which evoke ideas or images of things in people's minds. Over time these ideas or images become familiar or established in society and therefore become identities for the products or companies they represent. One only has to see the graphic symbol (or logo) to trigger the image of the company or product in his mind. In the above example from the Bible, Jesus is the symbol or logo for Christianity.

There are many ways to design logos. Most people think the only way is to draw a realistic or simplified picture of the product. If you are a library, then you draw a book. If you sell coffee, then you draw a picture of a steaming cup of hot coffee. If you're a carpenter, then you draw a picture of a hammer or some other carpenter's tool.

But even though that is one of the techniques, there are other methods to design logos. In this chapter we'll discuss some of the ways. People are constantly breaking the rules and redefining the parameters of design, so I can't say that we'll discuss ALL the ways of designing logos. But here are some techniques to get you started:

> Abstract Symbols of Real Things
> Logotype of the Business Name
> Letterforms
> Illustrative – Real and Cartoon
> Non-Objective Designs
> Use of Various Shapes
> Combinations of Techniques

Abstract Symbols of Real Things

The most obvious approach to designing logos is to take real things and simplify them into graphic symbols. This is usually done by eliminating all the details and transforming the thing into a geometric-like shape. It therefore becomes a stylized depiction of the real thing, but nevertheless is still recognizable for what it represents.

For example, the oval below with the family inside it represents the lifestyle and values of people in America's heartland. These are people who farm the land. The head of the house looks as if he is protecting his family and his land from danger. The boy is holding a book, which could be the Bible or a home schooling book. The logo belongs to American Christian Ministries.

In the case of the Del E. Webb Memorial Hospital, located in Phoenix, Arizona, the graphic artists chose not to depict a hospital or anything medical, which, by its very nature, is negative, because it deals with sick people. Instead, we focused on the idea of the legendary Phoenix bird and ended up shaping it into the letter "W."

American Christian Ministries

American Health Resorts

Alpha Bee Service

Picture This Modeling Agency

Logotype of the Business Name

Sometimes, as you work on a logo design, you can't think of anything to illustrate. Sometimes just designing some interesting typestyle using the words of the business name can be enough to form a logo.

The examples below show that you can use just about any technique to create what's known as a "Logotype." And there are hundreds of design techniques for manipulating letterforms. You can employ handlettering with bold swashes as in the KNNN radio station logotype. Or you can "illustrate" the letters as in the Hot Knots logotype. Or you can employ many other ways to design a logotype.

All you have to do is pay attention to the techniques designers use already and you'll discover that they can be collected, categorized and easily referenced when you're brainstorming for an idea. You will even find that certain techniques are used over and over by different designers.

Letterforms

Another approach you can take in your quest for a creative logo design is to just focus on the first letter of the word or words of the business name. You can just design an interesting letter or letters or you can combine abstract symbols with the letterforms to communicate what the business is about as in the jet airplane in the Air Courier logo or the record and tape reel in Churchill Productions logo.

Rejected logo for Air Couriers

Another rejected logo for Air Couriers

Rejected logo for
Churchill Productions Recording Studio

Rejected logo for Bostwick Construction

Illustrative - Real & Cartoon

In certain cases a realistic illustration or cartoon can evoke a certain image where any other approach can't. Take the Granada Pitching Machines Logo, for instance. How do you give a mechanical baseball pitching machine an exciting image in a logo? Even though it's a good machine, just illustrating the machine itself doesn't evoke the kind of excitement the product warrants. So you add something to it. You add something that DOES evoke excitement: a drawing of a REAL baseball player. And if you put him inside the machine, then the message of what the machine does is communicated. Of course, it's easier to put a cartoon baseball player inside a machine, because anything is possible with cartoons.

On other logo design assignments, realistic drawings are more appropriate. In the High Profiles Modeling Agency logo the eye is a traditional attention-getter, but when it's a female eye it also effectively represents glamour and, thus, modeling.

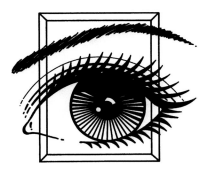

High Profiles Modeling Agency

Granada Pitching Machines

Touvelle House Bed & Breakfast

Fowl Ball Creations

Non-Objective Designs

On a purely right-brained level product identification comes down to just a recognizable mark. After all the left-brained rationalizations, justifications and explanations about a company's logo have been removed, the visual "mark" is only what the public sees and remembers. So why not design a purely non-objective geometrical design with no story or explanation of words to back it up? Once it has been around for a while, it will become established and people will know what it is anyway.

The problem with this approach is that most clients aren't art-oriented or right-brain friendly, so they'll think this approach doesn't make any sense. But it is just as viable an approach to logo design as any other. Do a little research project and look at all the non-objective logo designs that are out there. If you are lucky enough to find a client who appreciates this approach, you'll have fun coming up with a design.

Use of Various Shapes

If your first attempts at a certain logo design don't look very exciting, try incorporating geometric or free-form shapes into the logo. For example, in the Crystal Fresh Bottled Water Logo below, the mountains of Oregon were framed by the shape of the state of Oregon. Then the name of the business was placed inside a curved shape with rounded ends. The gradients inside the picture are blue and green and all the outlines are blue.

In the Hardwood Creations Logo, the classic shapes of ribbons are used to create a special feel. They are combined with a circle, a square shape and a long, straight tubular shape to produce a single strong unit of design. Again, the type is placed inside the shapes.

Combinations of Techniques

When it comes to logo design, any approach is legitimate. Just make sure the logo reproduces well when it is any size, especially a small size in an ad or on a letterhead. Also make sure it reproduces well when it is reproduced in color OR black and white. The effect your logo produces should be one of strength and boldness because you want it to stand out and be seen in the sea of graphic design.

Then just mix and match techniques to obtain new designs. And don't just think that the techniques I have mentioned are the only ones. As time goes on, trends come and go and the rules seem to always be broken again and again. So use the techniques I have mentioned to build on and go on to invent your own approaches based on recombining the gimmicks, techniques and styles of other current graphic designers.

Maybe you notice that a certain graphic designer used reverse type with a gradient background in a logo, but you can see a better way to use the same technique. Then all you have to do is place the whole thing in an interesting geometric shape, use a drop shadow or place an abstract symbol that conveys what the business does and lo and behold, you have a new, creative logo!

The Hot One logo combines a basic circle Shape with Abstract flame forms, that also define the edges of the Logotype.

The Bostwick Logo combines a 3D Logotype design with a simplified Illustrative rendering of house framework.

The Deer Creek Vineyards logo makes use of the Logotype combined with an Abstract treatment of grapes combined with antlers and leaves to represent a deer head.

THE GRAPHIC DESIGN POLICE

Fighting Design Crime Wherever It Rears Its Ugly Head

On April 20, 1994 the Graphic Design Police surrounded Clud's Copy Service and held him at bay for several hours until he finally gave up, fortunately without spilling a drop of ink. Cludamus Farkle had committed an *897: Using multiple confusing names and logos for a single business.* Besides "Clud's Copy Service" some people knew the business as "Clud's, A Complete Service Printer." Some knew it as "Clud's Copies & Printing." Other names were "Clud the Printer" and "Clud's Printing." Because of this confusing use of logos and names, on any given day of the week there were always dazed and confused people stumbling around and bumping into each other outside the establishment. Finally the GDP came down on Cludamus Farkle and threw him in the clink without hope of kerning, right justification or a work and turn setup.

Cludamus Farkle

Clud's
A COMPLETE SERVICE PRINTER

EXHIBIT A:
Here are the various logos Farkle used to advertise his business. Besides the name variations, all the logos are totally different from each other. As a result, there is no single strong image conveyed to the public. The sign on the building has one logo; the business card has another logo; the letterhead has still another logo; the notepads have even another logo!

Clud's Copy Service

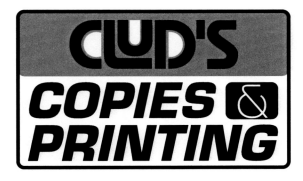

EXHIBIT B:
Farkle was given a stern lecture by the judge and after he was released, he immediately re-registered the name of his business and had a new, up-to-date Logo designed. Farkle even stopped wearing his baseball cap backwards.

Design Projects

1. Look through old magazines and newspapers for any and all logos you can find. Keep in mind the different categories of logos you have read about in this chapter and try to get 5 or more different logos to fill each category. Be sure to include the business name if the logo doesn't have it in it. As you collect these examples, notice the techniques and gimmicks the designers have used to design their logos. Notice how they are similar to the examples you see in this book, but also notice how they are different than the examples you see in this book. You should be collecting the logos that appeal to you. Get 7 pages and label the top of each page after the 7 categories discussed in this chapter. Paste your 5 or more examples of Abstract Symbols of Real Things on the first page and so on until you have pasted up all your logo examples on all 7 pages. Once you have done this you will have some reference material not only on the page but also in your mind for project 2 and beyond.

2. Now choose any one of your example logos you have cut out of magazines and newspapers and redesign it using a different category of approach. In other words, if you find a logo that is mainly an Abstract symbol, try to work with just the Logotype of the Business Name. Or take a logo that has a Realistic Illustrative drawing and design a completely Non-Objective design for it. Use whatever tools you are comfortable with: do rough pencil sketches, or use a T-square, compass and triangle on a drawing board, or just use a draw program to build your design on a computer. Redesign the logo using all 7 categories, trying to make sure you like each example when you're finished designing it. In real life you have to be able to come up with 3 to 5 different approaches fast and the client usually picks the logo you like the least. (It's called "Murphy's Law.") So if you like all your examples, then, no matter which one he picks, you'll have fun doing the finished rendering.

3. Pretend that Mom, Dad, Sister or Brother is the client. Have one of them select one of your 7 logos that will be used for the final logo. You'll have a great feeling of accomplishment if they choose the logo idea you like. But be prepared; more times than I care to think about, the client didn't like my "precious" and wonderful idea. They liked my "okay" idea down the list about 3 examples. Or they might start combining two of your ideas to try and improve on your logo designs. Sometimes this works. Sometimes it doesn't. Remember, if you have thrown away all the logo ideas you really didn't think were that good, then you'll still be excited about doing a finished rendering of the logo the client picked. Once the choice is made, create a business card with the logo on it, or design a small newspaper ad with the logo in the ad. The copy for the ad is not important at this point. Just make the business card or ad look nice.

Important Things To Remember

1. The word "logo" derives from the ancient Greek word "logos." What is the true meaning of the word "logos?"

2. Over time graphic symbols establish the _____ of a company or product they represent.

3. What is the most common way people use to design a logo?

4. What is the term for a logo that is composed of just the company name designed with an interesting type style?

5. What is the term for a logo that has no recognizable symbol or picture and no story or explanation of words to back it up?

6. List 3 important things your originally designed logo should do:

   a. _____

   b. _____

   c. _____

7. True or False: The techniques mentioned in this chapter are the best techniques for creating logos.

Answers on page 98

Answers

1. The true meaning of the word "logos" is communication.

2. Over time graphic symbols establish the IDENTITY of a company or product they represent.

3. The most common method people use to design a logo is to draw a realistic or simplified picture of the product. This can be accomplished by using 2 of the techniques discussed in this chapter: Abstract Symbols of Real Things and Illustrative – Real & Cartoon.

4. The term for a logo that is composed of just the company name designed with an interesting type style is LOGOTYPE.

5. The term for a logo that has no recognizable symbol or picture and no story or explanation of words to back it up is NON-OBJECTIVE.

6. List 3 important things your originally designed logo should do:

   a. Reproduce well at any size – small or large.

   b. Reproduce well in color OR black & white.

   c. Be bold so that it stands out from all the other graphic design out there.

7. False: The logo creation techniques mentioned in this chapter, while good, might not be considered the best techniques for creating logos by some graphic designers. Since design trends come and go and there is always someone out there who breaks a design rule, which then becomes popular, you should only use the techniques discussed in this chapter as an entry point. After that, see what other current graphic designers are doing and combine and recombine their gimmicks, techniques and styles until you come up with a winning logo.

DESIGN RULES

Once you know about all the design tools (design elements) and the structure of a page, you have to learn HOW to use these tools on the page. The design rules are the broader concepts that guide you in the use of the specific design tools. This chapter will explain more about them. They are:

> Dominance
> Repetition
> Rhythm
> Unity
> Contrast
> Gradation
> Balance

As you play lines against shapes, space against colors, values against textures and etc., you should look for how well your whole layout follows the design rules. Sure, you have diligently employed the elements of design in your layout, but is there enough dominance, balance, contrast or etc. exhibited? If you not only use the design tools but also follow the design rules, your layouts will look more appealing and more professional.

In your study of the different rules, you will find that they overlap. Repetition is part of rhythm and also contributes to unity and gradation. And the proper use of dominance, contrast and repetition creates balance.

It might take a while for you to see how these rules all work in each one of your unique designs, but if you know what to look for, then you'll have a better chance at creating a good design.

Dominance

The whole idea behind dominance is that you must have a hierarchy of importance to all the elements of your layout. One element has to be the most important and one has to be the least important with all the other elements in between – one being a little more important than the other. For instance, in the ad for the made-up organization, *ParadigmShifters*, shown on this page, there is a typical hierarchy that occurs in many good ads. The photo is the most dominant thing, followed by the headline, followed by the sub-copy (in this case the quotes), followed by the block of body copy below the photo. Finally, there is the logo, followed by the address and phone. If you were to change the relative sizes of these elements so that they were all about equal in size and weight, as shown on the next page, then your layout would become dull and uninteresting because all the elements would be competing with each other for the position of "focal point." Consequently, there would be no dominance, no focal point and thus, no punch. Elements on a page naturally want to be sorted into a hierarchy of importance. This creates balance.

A good layout has a focal point where the eye is drawn first above all other places in the ad or composition. The focal point is usually the dominant or emphasized element in your layout. This is usually created when one element differs from the rest in size, color, line, texture, or etc. As we saw in chapter one, you can emphasize type by making it bold, underlining it, making it in italics, making it all caps, or printing it in a color like red instead of just plain black. On a page with many rectangular photos you can make your most important photo a circular photo.

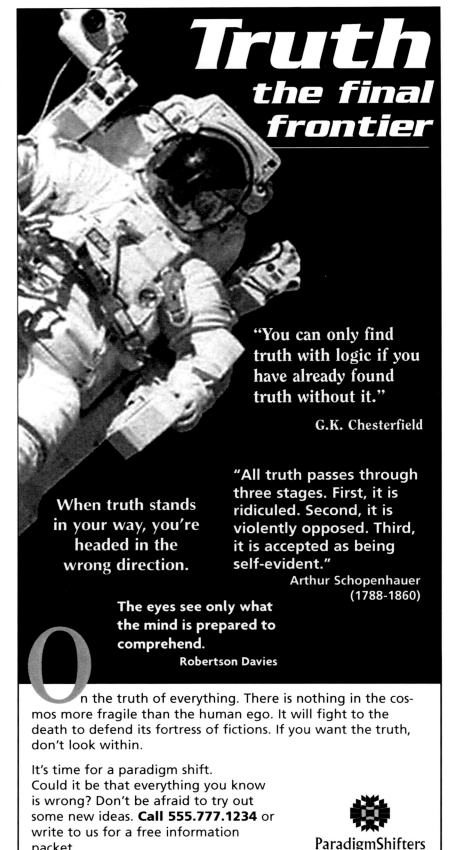

Truth
the final frontier

"All truth passes through three stages. First, it is ridiculed. Second, it is violently opposed. Third, it is accepted as being self-evident."

Arthur Schopenhauer
(1788-1860)

The eyes see only what the mind is prepared to comprehend.

Robertson Davies

"You can only find truth with logic if you have already found truth without it."

G.K. Chesterfield

When truth stands in your way, you're headed in the wrong direction.

On the truth of everything. There is nothing in the cosmos more fragile than the human ego. It will fight to the death to defend its fortress of fictions. If you want the truth, don't look within.

It's time for a paradigm shift. Could it be that everything you know is wrong? Don't be afraid to try out some new ideas. **Call 555.777.1234** or write to us for a free information packet.

ParadigmShifters
123 Cosmos Drive
Oshfurt, Oregon

In the first ad on the left the focal point is the astronaut, which, because of his tilt, points you right at the headline, the next most important element of the ad. Because of the variation on the Star Trek theme, your curiosity is aroused and you want to read down the ad to find out what this headline is all about.

As you compare the two ads, notice that the area of black in the second ad is the same size as the area of white — something that causes visual conflict. It also makes the reader think there are two ads instead of just one. On the other hand there's no doubt that the area of black in the ad on the left is the dominant area and not the white area. The initial cap "O," by overlapping from the white area onto the black area, also ties the two background areas together.

Also, notice in the ad on the right that all the type is about the same size. Sure, you read down the ad the same as in the ad on the left, but your eye keeps jumping around among the various elements subconsciously trying to decide which one is more important. The ad on the right ends up being "scattered" looking and weak, whereas the ad on the left ends up having visual power because of the careful application of a hierarchy of dominance.

Repetition

Things that repeat occur around us all the time. For instance, the slats in the blinds in the window present a repetitious display of horizontal lines. As you drive down the street you see street light poles repeating themselves at regular intervals all along the sidewalk. The human eye notices all this repetition on a conscious and unconscious level.

The blinds in the window and the light poles on the street are usually seen on an unconscious level because they represent endless repetition, which tends to become boring or even hypnotic if overdone. But if you see one or two bent slats in the blinds or if one light pole is missing in the long line along the road, then your eyes take notice right away. This eye-catching effect is what is known as "repetition with variation," and you can include this design rule in your layouts to make them more interesting. Repeat objects of clip art on a page but make them each slightly different in design color or size and you have used repetition with variation.

Repetition can create a visual rhythm the same way a repetitive beat in a song creates an audio rhythm. Repetition also creates unity. When you employ the same 3-column grid on every page of a newsletter with repeating subheads set in the same typeface, this tends to tie together the whole newsletter.

If you're having trouble making your design exciting or interesting, look for consistent elements in the content that you could exaggerate into repeating design elements. And if you can't find any consistent elements to repeat, force the principle of repetition into your layout by adding unrelated designs or drawings that repeat.

Repetition with variation can also be used to create a sense of movement in your layout. Movement always adds interest. You can create the illusion of movement by showing the sequential frames of an animated cartoon figure or you can show time passing by displaying a series of pictures showing a flower blooming.

In the example below of a magazine contents page, notice how there is repetition of the same sized photos lined up right next to each other. The descriptive text repeats by being all set the same. A touch of variation is added by putting one photo on the bottom row instead of on the top row. And even though all the page numbers are the same size and type style, one of them is positioned at the top of the photo instead of at the bottom. These slight variations make all the repetition more interesting.

CONTENTS

Anger Management
One company is bottling it up and selling it.
BY BOINCH UPZ

Smooth Skin
What is it? How do you get it? Interviews with 3 circus elephants
BY ENYA FACE

A Walk in the Park
Why is it so easy? Is it like a cake walk? Is it easier than falling off a log? The controversial views.
BY JACK RIPPER

Heavy Animals
The reasons why overweight animals don't worry about their weight.
BY ORSON CLOBA

Washing Dishes
Experts say that the first thing you have to do is get rid of dirt.
BY ROBERTA SMUDGE

Important Safeguards

When using electrical appliances, especially around children, you should always follow basic safety precautions including the following:

Read all instructions before using
Keep away from water

Danger - Any appliance is electrically live even when the switch is off. To reduce the risk of death by electric shock:

1. Always unplug it immediately after using.
2. Do not use while bathing or in a shower.
3. Do not place or store appliance where it can fall or be pulled into a tub or sink full of water.
    4. Do not place in, or drop into, water or other liquid.
      5. If an appliance falls into water, unplug it immediately. Do not reach into the water.

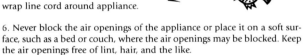

Warning: To reduce the risk of burns, electrocution, fire, or injury to persons:

1. This appliance should never be left unattended when plugged in.

2. Close supervision is necessary when this appliance is used by, on or near children or invalids.

3. Use this appliance only for its intended use as described in this manual. Do not use attachments not recommended by the manufacturer.

4. Never operate this appliance if it has a damaged cord or plug, if it is not working properly, if it has been dropped or damaged, or dropped into water. Return the appliance to an authorized service center for examination and repair.

5. Keep the cord away from heated surfaces. Do not pull, twist, or wrap line cord around appliance.

6. Never block the air openings of the appliance or place it on a soft surface, such as a bed or couch, where the air openings may be blocked. Keep the air openings free of lint, hair, and the like.

7. Never use while sleeping.

8. Never drop or insert any object into any opening or hose.

In this example notice how the fish repeat themselves in size and similar shape but are obviously all different (repetition with variation). We started with some boring text and then forced some somewhat unrelated repeating graphics into the layout to make it more interesting.

It might be difficult to actually get a client to agree to forcing clip art that really doesn't relate into a layout to make it more interesting. But sometimes, depending on the subject matter and the client, if you take a chance, your client will like this -what he thinks- is a new, different approach to layout design.

The repeating caveman in the example below is given variation by turning the last caveman upside down. You can use this technique to show how someone stands out from the crowd or is different in a positive or negative way.

HOW TO HANDLE **THE DIFFICULT CLONE**

Rhythm

Normally, rhythm is associated with music. A sonata has a slow, relaxing rhythm and a Sousa march has a faster-paced, rigid rhythm. But rhythm can be visual, also. If the letters in a line of type are randomly positioned above or below the baseline, a fun, informal rhythm is created. A regular rhythm can be made by repeating the same-sized and shaped photos in a row, evenly spaced along the same baseline.

So, as you can see, the design rule of repetition plays an integral part in the design rule of rhythm. The illusion of motion can be created with the aid of a fast rhythm by employing sweeping, curving lines or tilting a picture of a train, plane or car.

So when you are planning your design, you want to think about the mood you want to evoke in the reader. Just as the rhythm of the music fits the action in a movie, likewise the visual rhythm in your layout fits the subject of your layout. You can create a wild, exciting mood or a calm, relaxing one based on the type of visual rhythm you choose.

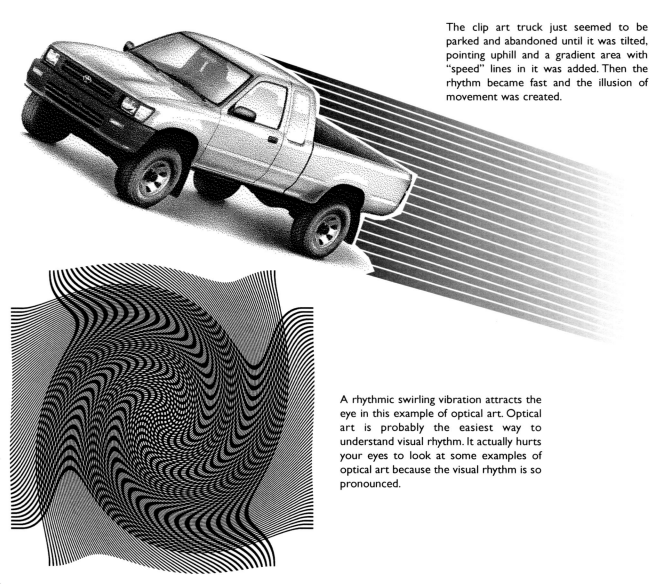

The clip art truck just seemed to be parked and abandoned until it was tilted, pointing uphill and a gradient area with "speed" lines in it was added. Then the rhythm became fast and the illusion of movement was created.

A rhythmic swirling vibration attracts the eye in this example of optical art. Optical art is probably the easiest way to understand visual rhythm. It actually hurts your eyes to look at some examples of optical art because the visual rhythm is so pronounced.

'Twas brillig, and the slithy toves
Did gyre and gimble in the wabe;
All mimsy were the borogoves,
And the mome raths outgrabe.

The rhythm of the words from Lewis Carroll's *Jabberwocky* become whimsical and carefree when they are placed on curving baselines in this design.

TABLE OF CONTENTS

The exact spacing and repetition of lines between the numbers in the table of contents to the left creates a familiar rhythm seen in old car radios and speedometers – an interesting way to handle a table of contents!

When your client gives you a word or subject that is unexciting, you can raise the visual excitement factor by giving the type not only three dimensions, but sweeping and curving lines as in the example below. The rhythm of shooting upward movement is created. Also the rhythm of a flash of light or explosion is created by the jagged lines surrounding the type.

Unity

Unity is good because there is a state of harmony when there is unity. In a group of people if everyone is thinking along the same lines, everybody is happy. If everyone in the group has different views, then there are arguments and conflict. People are not happy and they want to leave.

When architects design a building, they follow a set of guidelines that become known as "the style" for that building. All the windows share a certain design that fits that style. The hallways and doors all fit the same design criteria. As a result, when people are inside the building, they are comfortable with the unity of design and want to stay. If a building is designed with absolutely no unity, then it looks weird. As people walk through the building, they don't know what to expect. Each window and door is a different design. The height of the ceilings in each room is different. The design is a hodgepodge and clutter of everything, which is too much for the eye to take in all at once. People want to leave.

The same is true of graphic design. If you have a clutter of all kinds of fonts, art styles and information in your layout, you will chase your reader away. But sometimes it's hard NOT to have a clutter of many different things in an ad or layout. So you have to unify the clutter to make it easier on the reader's eyes.

Repetition of similar design elements is one way to unify a layout. Use the same font for every subhead and blurb. Use the same-size and shaped box for every different product. In a newsletter covering diverse subject matter use the same 3-column grid for every page.

How can you possibly unify a hot dog, a piano and a motorcycle? They are three vastly contrasting objects! In the example below they become unified when they are put on a common background. Also notice how they are all light and open with little shading. That not only makes them stand out on the background, but also makes them look similar in style. They are also "cut out" of their original backgrounds so that they are all floating on the new background. With all these common details the reader senses that they are somehow all tied together.

In the department store signs to the right notice how they all look like they belong together. First, they are all the same size and shape of sign. Second, they all have an identical grid pattern as a background. Third, the same thickness of outline and simple style is employed in depicting each object. Fourth, every object is cropped so you don't see the entire object. Fifth, the same type font is used in every sign. The store logo could also be added on each sign as one more common element of unity.

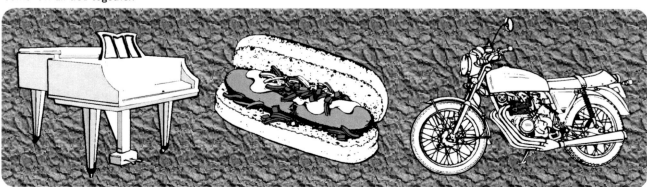

Here is a circumstance where the designer had many different things to include in the layout. Notice how he put them on a common background and how he used similar type in each oval. Also notice how all the same-size ovals have the same style – the out-of-register dotted line on top of the white oval. Whenever you have an ad with many elements, it's good to incorporate a lot of sameness into everything to tie it all together.

Contrast

With unity, consistency and sameness were the key words. Contrast is the opposite of unity; you are *trying* to make things look different. Too much unity, just as too much repetition, can be boring. Contrast is like a spice; it can be added to spark up an otherwise dull layout. You can contrast any element of design. Put a thin line next to a really thick line. Put a circle next to a square. Put a black panel next to a white panel. Put a few small objects next to a very large object. Put a rough-textured area or object next to a smooth area or object. Put small type next to large type.

LIGHTS................................

CAMERA

..............ACTION

In the above example the contrast employed is in the size of the type. But if you only make the type slightly larger than the other type, then you don't really achieve contrast. The size difference has to be *really* blatant to succeed in contrasting.

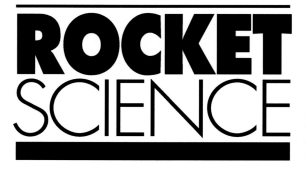

Not only does the heavy type contrast with the thin type, but the thin rule contrasts with the heavy rule in this type example.

Contrast of value is employed in this example by having the white type on black background juxtaposed with the black type on white background. You'll see this tried and true technique used often in graphic design.

On this project the designer redefined the problem from "What can I use to illustrate role playing?" to "How can I alter a photo of an actor to give the impression he's someone else?" By using the design rule of Contrast, the graphic designer rendered one half of the actor in a loose sketchy style with no grays which contrasts with the smooth, precise rendition of the grayscale photo. This is a contrast of texture.

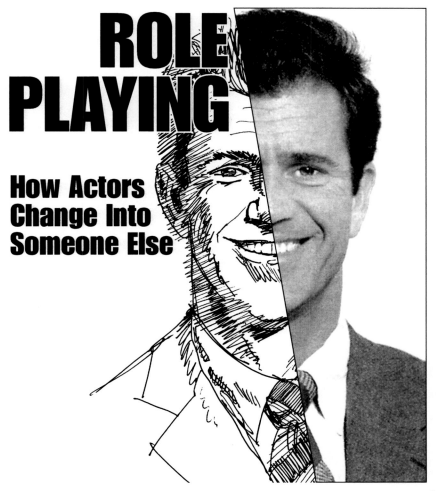

ROLE PLAYING

How Actors Change Into Someone Else

Gradation

A painting, drawing or design can always be improved by supplying the principle of Gradation. Gradation is a gradual change of any design tool in a composition and provides a smooth transition between areas of the design. Instead of having a hard edge to a photo, you can soften the effect by feathering the edge. The photo then gradually merges with its background. Instead of putting a flat background of color in an ad, put an airbrushed gradient background of color from dark to light or from a warm color to a cool color. When using lines as your chosen design tool, start with jagged lines and make them change gradually into smooth, straight lines. Make several rectangular shapes on a page gradually change into oval shapes.

Whenever you use gradation in a design, it takes on a much more sophisticated, subtle look. If your subject is about growth, change or transition of some sort, gradation can be employed to convey that subject better.

Horizontal lines gradually change from thin to thick in this type example illustrating high-speed movement

In the example below gradation has been combined with texture. The texture is the use of coarse halftone dots which gradually change from big dots to small dots, thus creating the gradation. The thick black outlines and various areas of solid black help define the rose amongst the busy pattern of dots.

Make owning your dream car a reality!

The gradual fade-in of the car in the sequence above simulates a simple visual effect that you would normally expect to see in a movie or on TV. In this example, the use of gradation also overlaps another design rule: repetition with variation.

Notice how the various gradients all go from dark to light in different directions in the type at the left. There is also a gradient background behind the type and in front of the type there are "swinging" transparent arcs that have gradients inside them as well.

The example below employs a simple "storyboard" technique to show gradual change of a flower. Even though the concept of "change" is a different way of thinking about gradation, it is still another approach to the idea of using gradation in a layout.

the spirit is growing!

Balance

Balance comes into play in more than just thinking of our own balance when we stand, walk, or run. It occurs in cooking where you have to have the right amounts of different ingredients to create a balance that results in a dish that tastes good. Balance affects interpersonal relationships where a balance of give and take creates amiable feelings between two people. In music, a balance of high-pitched and low-pitched instrument sounds and fast and slow segments of music create a pleasing melody. And even in graphic design, one element affects another in a layout. By changing the color, value, size, shape and texture of the various elements in your layout, you can affect the balance of the entire layout.

In the style of balance called *symmetry*, all the elements are centered horizontally and vertically. This is a good style for a subject that is very traditional, formal, and established. Another style of balance is called *asymmetry*, where all the elements are off-centered but still balanced. This style is good when you want to evoke variety, informality, movement, and fun in a layout.

You can achieve balance in an asymmetrical layout by careful positioning of all the elements based on their "weight" and how they relate to each other on the page. A dark area of the layout is balanced by placing it opposite a similar-sized light area.

Alignment is also a very important aspect of balance. For example, if you hang many elements along a common invisible line, your layout will tend to balance itself. Alignment can also create movement and movement can balance a layout.

In the example of "The Players" all the pictures are made of a uniform size and "hung" from the common line created by the black bar at the top of the layout. This unity of size and alignment creates balance for this layout. The type below each picture is in a left-justified column, that is the same width as the picture, so that each picture and its type is like a banner hanging from the ceiling. It doesn't matter that each block of text differs in length because everything is balanced by the alignment at the top of the layout.

The Players

Drawings by Adam Bunch

While waiting in line for a department store to open, she spills some coffee on a skunk that just happens along, causing a riot in the street.

This idiot savant solved the physics problem Einstein failed to solve while at the same time discovering a way not to lose his socks in the washing machine.

The contract killer no one liked stepped off a cruise ship into an oil spill as a dirigible carrying a load of goose down feathers exploded in the sky far above.

She lost her pet skunk while on an Alaskan cruise ship around an oil spill created when Einstein failed to solve a physics problem. In a fit of emotion she decided to open a department store.

The nerd who successfully hacked his way into the complex mainframe of an international computer consortium only to discover that Dan's Donut Den didn't sell coconut-coated, chocolate-blasted jelly rolls.

This disgruntled restaurant waitress spilled some coffee on a skunk who just happened to order a Spanish omelette after narrowly escaping a riot in the street.

This guy was in the bookstore the whole time reading a comic book about the Migraine Men vs. Dr. Garbanzo and His Exploding Beard of Doom.

Redesigning Dinosaurs

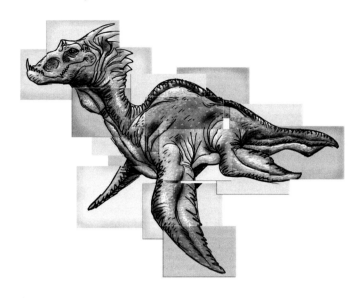

HOW WE HAVE CHANGED OUR PERCEPTION OF PREHISTORIC CREATURES

redesigning dinosaurs

HOW WE HAVE
CHANGED OUR
PERCEPTION OF
PREHISTORIC
CREATURES

The two examples on this page show how the same project can be arranged into a symmetrical layout and an asymmetrical layout.

In the top symmetrical layout the headline, illustration, and subhead are all centered horizontally and vertically. The objective is to make everything as formal and traditional as possible, even to the point of capitalizing the first letter in the words of the headline. Also notice how the entire illustration is shown.

In the bottom, asymmetrical layout there is more informality displayed. This is accomplished by making all the letters in the headline a non-traditional lower case and providing contrast by having one word in thin type and the other word in heavy type.

Also, nothing is centered, but the elements do align to bring balance to the layout. The word "redesigning" aligns with the edge of the first rectangle of the illustration. The word "dinosaurs" nests directly into the notch created by two composited rectangles of the illustration .

The subhead balances the headline by being on the other side of the illustration with the dinosaur's head in between. Notice how the bottom of the second line of the subhead aligns with the bottom of the rectangle of the illustration.

Asymmetry is enhanced by having only a part of the illustration in the layout. And the heavy black space of the word "dinosaurs" is balanced by placing white space above and below it.

On October 6, 2001 the GDP was called to the scene of a typographical conflict in progress at Alorius Packertrain's Graphic Design Studio. It seems as if an innocent bystander accidentally wandered into Packertrain's studio, looked over her shoulder and witnessed a traumatic sight on her computer screen. According to the witness, Packertrain was attempting to employ the principle of contrast in a headline, but instead foolishly ended up with conflict. Thinking quickly under pressure the witness dialed the Graphic Design Emergency number and then began screaming. Seconds later 15 GDP officers had to rappel down the side of the building and crash through Packertrain's office window—one at a time —to gain entry to the studio before any more damage was done. Packertrain is now in custody and the witness escaped with minor injuries.

Alorius Packertrain

How will the

extinction of all life

as we know it

affect the way we view the cosmos

?

EXHIBIT A:
Here is the illegal headline Packertrain was working on. Notice how the middle two lines of type are only slightly different in style and size. It almost looks like a typesetting mistake. The question mark is larger in size, but not by much. Not only does the whole design look like a mistake, but it also looks timid, uncertain and conflicting.

How will the

EXTINCTION OF ALL LIFE
AS WE KNOW IT

affect the way we view the cosmos

EXHIBIT B:
After Packertrain went through three months of typographic rehabilitation here is the revised design she came up with for the same headline. Now there is no question about the middle two lines being in contrast to the other two lines. Not only is the type bigger and much bolder, but all the letters have been capitalized. Also the question mark has become a very contrasting gigantic design motif in the background.

Design Projects

1. Find an ad in a newspaper or magazine that is a certain size. The size could be approximately 6 inches by 5 inches or 8 inches by 10 inches – it doesn't matter. The point is to settle on a specific size and then design your own ad. Pretend you are in a certain kind of business you like. Maybe you're selling Teddy bears or maybe you have a Sports Store where you sell skateboards or baseball equipment. Figure out all the elements that you want in your ad: photos, illustrations, headlines, body copy, logo, etc. Give your company a name and come up with a logo. Or if you can't think of anything along those lines, find an existing ad with all the proper elements and redesign it. First design your ad so that all the elements are in symmetrical balance. Then design a second ad – the same size – where all the same elements are in asymmetrical balance. You can either use a computer to do this or you can draw pictures by hand using pencil, paper and a ruler. If you build your ad using paper and pencil, you can resize your different elements by making photocopies at a copy center and then cut everything out and paste it onto another piece of paper with a carefully drawn border for the ad.

2. Again, create an ad that is a certain size. Try to come up with a new, original layout. Don't just copy what someone else has already done. Just like in the first exercise you can either design your ad on a computer or do it by hand using pencil and paper. First, design your ad, trying hard to make every element approximately the same size. If you are doing an ad with pencil and paper, you can size things using a photocopy machine. Second, redesign the same ad, trying hard to size every element according to a hierarchy of predominance. Have one element be the focal point or the largest in size and then make each element smaller until your last element is the smallest in size. It will be up to you to figure out which elements are more important than the others.

3. Collect 5 ads or page layouts from magazines, newspapers and brochures that exemplify each of the design rules:
    Dominance
    Repetition
    Rhythm
    Unity
    Contrast
    Gradation
    Balance
Write or type a short paragraph for each example explaining which design rule it exemplifies—why and how.

Important Things To Remember

1. The whole idea of having dominance in your layout is that you must have a _____.

2. Where is the eye drawn first above all other places in a good layout or composition?

3. Endless repetition can become boring. What is the term for making endless repetition more interesting?

4. Which of the following design rules can be created using the rule of repetition? A. Movement, B. Unity, C. Rhythm, D. All of the above.

5. What is the best style of art that helps you understand visual rhythm?

6. Rhythm affects the _____ of your visual layout.

7. What is a good way to unify a layout with many different clashing elements?

8. Too much unity can be boring just like too much repetition. What tool can you use to counteract unity?

9. Besides the value of an area of a layout going from dark to light what else can be considered "gradation?"

10. What is symmetrical balance in a layout?

11. What is asymmetrical balance in a layout?

12. What three things can bring balance to an asymmetrical layout?

Answers on page 117.

Answers

1. *Dominance involves a hierarchy of importance of all the elements in your layout. One element is the most important. Another element is second in priority and so on down the line until the least important element.*

2. *The eye is first drawn to the Focal Point of a layout or composition because it is the dominant or emphasized element in the layout.*

3. *The term for making endless repetition more interesting is "repetition with variation." Repeat design elements on a page but make some of them slightly different in design color or size and you have used repetition with variation.*

4. *Repetition can be instrumental in creating movement, unity and rhythm. Many of the design rules overlap. Repetition is part of rhythm and also contributes to unity and gradation. And the proper use of dominance, contrast and repetition creates balance.*

5. *Optical Art is the best style of art that helps you understand visual rhythm. Because the visual rhythm is so pronounced, it actually hurts your eyes to look at some examples.*

6. *Rhythm affects the mood of your visual layout. You can create a fun, informal, regular, fast, wild, exciting or a calm, relaxing mood based on the type of rhythm you use.*

7. *A good way to unify a layout with many different clashing elements is to look for or introduce similar and repeating design elements to tie it all together.*

8. *The tool that counteracts unity is contrast. You look for design elements that look different than each other and then exaggerate their difference. The more exaggerated the difference the more the contrast.*

9. *Besides the value of an area of a layout going from dark to light, gradation is a gradual change of ANY design tool (line, shape, size, space, color, value, and texture) in a composition and provides a smooth transition between areas of the design.*

10. *Symmetrical balance in a layout is where all the elements are centered horizontally and vertically. Symmetrical balance is usually used with traditional subjects.*

11. *Asymmetrical balance in a layout is where all the elements are off-centered both vertically and horizontally but are still balanced. Asymmetrical balance is good for a fun, informal feeling and also can create movement.*

12. *The three things that can bring balance to an asymmetrical layout are 1. careful positioning of all the elements based on their "weight" and how they relate to each other on the page, 2. alignment, and 3. movement.*

7

HOW TO DESIGN A GOOD AD

Advertising and salesmen have gotten a bad image over the years. They are both perceived by many as an intrusive person getting in your face, trying to cram a product you don't necessarily want down your throat so they can make money off you. But that's the dark side of advertising and sales. Unfortunately, there ARE those salesmen and companies out there who are motivated by greed. But let's look at the marketplace with the motivation of customer service.

You have to make a living by selling your product or service, and let's say you develop a product that will genuinely help other people in some way. The first problem you'll encounter is that not everybody in the world wants or needs your product. You have to try to locate that cross-section (market segment) of society that has a need for the type of product you sell and put your ad in front of them, letting them know that you have it available for sale. The second problem you'll encounter is that when you've found the people who need the type of product you sell, you'll have to compete with other marketers who are trying to sell that same cross-section of people THEIR version of the same type of product.

So you can do one of two things: 1. You can make your product better for the customer than the other guy's product or 2. You can make your advertising gimmick more alluring than the other guy's. Obviously, you should make your product better, because you are honestly thinking about how you can help your customer. Your customers will appreciate your sincerity and you'll not only stay in business longer, but you'll get a good reputation. Of course, after you have improved your product, you can also use the second option. But if you choose the second option WITHOUT trying to improve your product, then you are thinking more about how much money you can make, rather than how you can serve your customer better. Unfortunately, there are both types of advertising in the marketplace and it's up to the customer to carefully research and choose between the sincere marketers and the greedy ones. Also, those customers that aren't interested will automatically "turn off," "tune out" or avoid that advertising that isn't aimed at them. And some people will simply tire of advertising in general and tune out all advertising.

In this chapter, we'll investigate some methods to get those customers you want to help and who are interested to respond to your ad once you have found them, rather than responding to your competitor's ad. Remember, prospective customers are those who, of their own free will, desire to purchase a product like yours; you're not trying to make *everyone* buy your product. "Finding" those people who want to buy a product like yours means –based on the scope of this book– they have discovered your ad in a magazine, newspaper or on the Internet. Now what do you do in your ad to get them to choose your product over your competitor's product? This chapter will tell you in more detail.

Solve a Problem.

If you show your reader how to solve a problem they have, you will immediately break down the salesmanship barriers, and you'll have a good chance at selling your product.

In the ad on this page a simple solution for the teenage problem of blackheads is suggested. It is appealing because it is promoted as a "quick fix" and the photo shows you immediately how it is used.

Use Emotion

Emotion is a very persuasive tool in selling ideas AND products. If you can make the reader relate to your product by stirring up emotions, then he will be more likely to buy your service or product.

Once the customer has been sold on your product or service, he or you can justify his choice with logic.

In the ad on this page people who have had frustrations with difficult people, whether they be bad customers, fellow employees, or family members, will relate to a basic urge to push a button that will immediately send the difficult person through a trap door in the floor.

Once the reader relates to that emotion, he is steered back to reality when the ad copy logically suggests that maybe there are better ways of dealing with conflicting interpersonal relationships. And, guess what? The Peacemakers, experts in conflict mediation and resolution, can show you what they are.

Don't you wish you could deal with jerks this way? Unfortunately, the upkeep on alligator pits and alligators is expensive these days. There are better ways of dealing with conflicts in interpersonal relationships. Let us show you how.

The Peacemakers
Conflict Mediation and Resolution
Call 5 5 5 - 6 7 8 4 Today

Think of the picture as a magnet

The idea in designing an ad is to get people to really look at your ad. Usually the first thing to do this is the graphic. If you put a lot of energy into creating an arresting photograph or graphic, you'll draw people into your ad. The graphic is what they remember after they turn the page.

In the example on this page a photo of a man has been altered in an exaggerated way until he is a caricature of his former self. The exaggerated features make the reader look at the ad twice to see what it's all about.

Humor sells

The ad on this page is also a good example of humor used to sell a product. The headline is so ironic in relation to the photo of the man, that you can't help but laugh. Even though humor is used in this ad in conjunction with a made-up product, you can still apply the techniques of humor to a real product or service. If you can make your ad fun, then it will be entertaining to the reader. A humorous ad is not only entertaining, but it is also catchy.

People like clever things and they like to laugh, so chances are they will be more likely to remember your ad and, as a result, buy your product.

More tips for creating a good ad

Make your reader feel good

Another approach to creating an ad is to make your readers feel good. Two examples where this technique is commonly used is with food products and entertainment such as movies, books, videos and video games. You can relieve the guilt most people feel about eating ice cream by explaining that your ice cream bar offers great taste and fewer calories in lower fat and no-sugar-added varieties that everyone can enjoy.

A video game ad can have a headline that says, "Experience the Excitement!" The young people it is aimed at feel good when they experience excitement, especially when they spend hours playing a favorite video game.

The headline is also a hook

It's also important to create a short, catchy headline that works in tandem with your graphic. Besides the eye-catching graphic, make the headline be another hook that lures the reader in, not just a repetition of what the graphic shows. Typeset it in a readable, yet intriguing font that's striking and complements the graphic.

It's amazing how many ads there are in print that don't take advantage of making the headline a hook. They simply make the name of the business the headline, as if their very name is enough to make people do a double take. This can make for a very dull ad that won't get many responses.

List the benefits of your product

Your potential customer wants to know what's in it for him. How will your product benefit him? But remember, when you are constructing your bulleted list of BENEFITS, make sure you aren't merely listing only the FEATURES of your product. There's a difference between features and benefits. Features can be important, because they are what generate the benefits, but the benefits to the customer are what really sell the product. It all comes down to how well you make life better and easier for your customer. If your product or service does it better than your competitor's, then the customer will buy your product or service instead of the other guy's.

Keep it simple

Many unskilled ad creators –mainly the owners of small businesses– make the mistake of putting too much text into their ads. They figure that if they are going to be paying such a high price for their advertisement in a newspaper or magazine, they had better try and cram as much information as possible into the small space. That way, they think, they'll get more for their money. But, often, when they do this, the reader is chased away because there is too much to read. Limit the theme of your ad to one thing and edit your verbiage so there are no unneeded words. If the reader wants to learn more, he can call you and ask.

Call to action

With the veritable sea of printed information out there, sometimes it's difficult to spur a reader into action. Maybe you have honestly found someone who's interested in the type of product or service you sell and you aren't trying to cram your product or service down some disinterested person's throat, against their will. But there still might be certain mental obstacles for that person to actually decide that they want to either come to your store or send for your product.

Maybe, they are just tired of the constant barrage of advertising, so they tune you out. Maybe they just haven't thought everything out to a logical conclusion and if your ad has action words in it, those words might be what complete their thought processes.

So, make sure you include verbs in either your headline or some other place in your ad. Use words and phrases such as: "*Call* today," "*Try* our new...," "*Take* advantage of...," or "*Buy* these...,"

Limited quantity, limited time

Sometimes using action words in your ad just isn't enough to get people to respond to your ad, come into your store, write, or call. Sometimes you have to create a sense of urgency by having a sale where you reduce the prices on your products for a limited time. A variation of this technique is to have a limited quantity of a certain product for sale. The technique of having a sale is of obvious benefit to the customer and shows you are trying to establish a rapport with them by giving them a discount once in a while.

Don't forget to be practical

After all the catchy headlines, alluring graphics, concise body text, simplicity and calls to action, don't forget about including your logo, name of business, location, phone number, web site address and other facts to help the customers respond to your ad.

THE GRAPHIC DESIGN POLICE

Fighting Design Crime Wherever It Rears Its Ugly Head

On June 21, 1997 an alert GDP officer observed a *6244 (Standard Really Bad Ad That Does Nothing)* happen when an innocent bystander opened a magazine and had his eyes glaze over upon seeing a really bad ad. If it hadn't been for the fact that the officer knew how to bring the victim out of acute Zombie Reader Psychosis, he could have been frozen there for days continually leafing through the magazine without a thought in his head.

The detectives traced the ad back to its creator, Dinka Doodat, a graphic designer who admitted she was in a hurry the day she created the ad. At her trial, the judge sentenced her to 2 years at hard labor – building ads without the aid of a computer.

Dinka Doodat

DREAD PIRATE ROBERT'S FURNITURE

"Real good furniture!"

123 E. MAIN STREET • 555-6789

EXHIBIT A:

Here's the standard really bad ad that the victim just happened to look at. Notice how the ad does nothing by assuming the standard structure of ads made by people who don't know that much about how to create ads. The name of the business is the headline and the graphic is just a photo or illustration of the building the owner is so proud of. You'd think he was trying to sell the building instead of furniture. There is no offer, no sale, no call to action or anything else to spur the reader to leave the house and come to the store.

Relax...
our easy chairs aren't
expensive

Come in and get an easy chair during "Couch Potato" week, July 11-18, and we'll knock 20% off the price of your chair!

DREAD PIRATE ROBERT'S FURNITURE
123 E. MAIN STREET
555-6789

EXHIBIT B:

After Doodat served her sentence, she was a changed graphic designer. She went back to her computer and came up with a headline that makes the reader feel good. It puts a sensory mental picture in the reader's mind about relaxing in an easy chair. And in the same headline, it gets the point across about a good easy chair not being expensive.

Then, on top of that, there is a specific call to action, telling the reader to "come in and get an easy chair." Also a sense of urgency is created by giving a 20% discount to customers for a limited time ("Couch Potato" week).

Design Projects

1. Just like in chapter 6, design your own ad of a business you have an interest in. If you want, it could be the same ad you used in the chapter 6 design project, or you can design a completely new and different ad. Make your first ad headline and body copy solve a problem for the reader. Design everything in the ad around this purpose. Design your second ad around the concept of using emotion to sell your product or service. Design your third ad around the concept of using an eye-catching graphic to lure your reader into the ad. Try humor as the driving force in your fourth ad. For the fifth ad layout, just make the readers feel good about themselves. As you can see, the idea is to go down the list of techniques and, using each as a focus, build an ad based on it. If you'd like, you could just sketch out the ads as you go. If it's hard for you to visualize the completed ad by just sketching, then take your time and build the ads on the computer or by carefully drawing them out. As you build your ads and write your copy, remember to make your headline a "hook" to pull readers in; keep your ad simple – don't put too many different themes or elements into it; clearly point out your benefits, not just your features; make sure you have a call to action; think about doing an ad that creates a sense of urgency by having a limited-time sale; be sure to include your logo, name, address, phone number, and website. When you are done, you will see that some concepts worked better with your product or service than others. From all these ads you've done you can pick the ad that works the best and go with it.

2. Look for an existing ad in a newspaper or magazine that uses the time-honored but not-quite-so-effective technique of using the name of the business as the headline and a picture of the company building to sell the product. Locally-done ads are usually a good source for this because small businessmen, who don't have that much experience in marketing, devise their own ads. Then, using this ad as a basis, redesign it into a more effective ad, employing any of the techniques you've learned about that fit the best.

Important Things To Remember

1. The motivation for selling a product or service in an ad should be:
   A. To make money
   B. To help people

2. In trying to advertise your product or service what should you do?
   A. You can make your product better for the customer than the other guy's product
   B. You can make your advertising gimmick more alluring than the other guy's.
   C. Both A and B.

3. List four techniques to make a better ad.

4. What's the best thing that will get people to look at your ad?

5. The headline of an ad should simply repeat what the graphic is saying.
   True or False

6. What is the difference between benefits and features of a product or service?

7. What is the danger in trying to get the most for your money by filling your ad with as much information about your product or service as possible?

8. Even if you have honestly found someone who's interested in the type of product or service you sell, what are some reasons why they still won't respond to your ad?

9. What are two things you can do to get people to respond to your ad?

10. What basic things should ALWAYS be in your ads?

Answers on page 127

Answers

1. If you choose A. To make money, then you'll end up sacrificing anything for the goal of making money – even customer service. If you choose B. To help people, then you'll end up sacrifice anything for the goal of helping people – even money. The choice should be obvious at this point, but there are people who make the choice of caring about money instead of people.

2. Improve your product or service, thinking of the customer first and the rest will follow. After you have improved your product, you can then make your advertising gimmick more alluring than the other guy's. But if you choose just to make clever advertising without trying to improve your product, then you are thinking more about how much money you can make, rather than how you can serve your customer better, and people will soon see through you and go elsewhere.

3. Four techniques you can employ to make a better ad are:
   A. Solve a problem
   B. Use Emotion
   C. Use Humor
   D. Make your reader feel good.

4. The best thing that will get people to look at your ad is an arresting graphic.

5. False. The headline of an ad should not just be a repetition of what the graphic depicts. The headline should enhance the picture and take it one step further to deliver your message.

6. The difference between benefits and features of a product or service is essentially, what's in it for the customer. You can list features all day long, but that won't sell people as well as listing how your product or service can help the customer feel better or achieve what he wants.

7. The danger in trying to get the most for your money by filling your ad with as much information about your product or service as possible is that you will be making your ad more complex than it should be and with information overload, you'll make your ad hard to read, thereby chasing the reader away. The best thing in designing an ad is to keep it as simple and easy to read as possible.

8. Even if you have honestly found someone who's interested in the type of product or service you sell, they still won't respond to your ad because maybe, they are just tired of the constant barrage of advertising, so they tune you out. Or maybe they just haven't thought everything out to a logical conclusion and if your ad has action words in it, those words might be what complete their thought processes.

9. Two things you can do to get people to respond to your ad are:
   1. Place a call to action in your ad by using word phrases such as "Call today," "Try our new...," "Take advantage of...," or "Buy these...,"
   2. Create a sense of urgency by having a sale where you reduce the prices on your products for a limited time or have a limited quantity of a certain product for sale.

10. The basic things you should always have in your ads are your logo, name of business, location, phone number, web site address and other important facts to help the customers respond to your ad.

8
GRAPHICS IN AND FOR ELECTRONIC PUBLICATION

D o not be alarmed; this chapter will have a different feel to it. This chapter has a large number of concepts associated specifically with the electronic publication (ePublishing) of graphic arts and related materials and will deal with some technical computer concepts. It is intended to just be an introduction, not a programmer's guide or a technical guide. It will give you a brief history and then an introduction to some tips, guidelines, standards, and other places to look for information, should you choose to delve deeper into the technical aspects of computers and computer graphics. Remember to keep the Internet Graphic Design Police off your back.

Electronic publishing is now used in all types of electronic media delivery systems: Internet, intranet, CD, DVD, eBooks, software, television, movies, games, Human Machine Interface (HMI) and more. This does not even cover the use of computers in all types of printed matter. As monitors become bigger, thinner, cheaper, and have higher resolutions, they are being used in all types of applications. Monitors deliver clear, crisp colored graphics for far less money than printing. With touch screen monitors, the monitor has become a control interface as well as a delivery system. The graphics can be interactive and integrated into the rest of the work. Hyperlinks can be used to move a user to new sections of a document or to add clarification, definition, and depth, or it can transport the user to different screens for equipment controls. ePublishing is considered an immersive delivery system. It can pull you in and have you interact with it. The only other media that is similar is the published book. People lose themselves in good printed books on a regular basis.

eBooks are here and they are getting better. At this time, I personally classify it as an emerging technology. They have some problems that are being addressed. I think that they will become popular at some point in time. eBooks are a blend of hardware and software. The hardware part is usually a hand held device that is not much bigger than your hand or about the size of a sheet of paper. The hardware has a built-in operating system that is programmed into a chip that is initiated when the eBook reader is turned on. The software part is the eBook or any document that follows the eBook standard data file that can be stored onto a compatible memory device or downloaded directly to the eBook hardware from sources like the Internet. There are organizations that are beginning to develop the standards that will help make this a viable delivery device for all types of documents, not just books. The development of formal eBooks standards is being led by large companies and associations such as: Adobe Systems Incorporated, Microsoft, Association of American Publishers, McGraw-Hill, Random House, Inc., and many more companies and associations. For standards, how to publish, and other information on eBooks, search the Internet. Some key words are

eBook, Open eBook Standards, eBook publishing, etc. Check out
http://www.openeBook.org/

Printed books are interactive; you have to turn the page, you can open
more than one at a time, they refer to one another, they are comfortable,
and you can use them for research. The only thing a book lacks is a
built in search feature and hypertext. Electronic publishing uses the
same rules and considerations as the printed word. It can add depth and
speed to the interactivity that a printed book cannot match. The reality
is this: it could be many years before eBooks replace printed books.
People simply love books as they are. The book has been virtually
unchanged since the Chinese produced the earliest known printed book
in about 868 AD. The Gutenberg press was not invented until 1450; the
press did not change the basic book design, it just made it faster.
ePublishing began to exist sometime between 1960 and 1970. It was
born with the Internet. The first eDocuments were ASCII or plain unformatted text. The documents were simply plain text documents and databases stored on large mainframe computers for the military and research
facilities (large universities and government operated the computers) to
share on what is known as ARPANET. No, what's his name did not
invent the Internet. In fact, I propose that no single person did. The
concept of the Internet and the way it works, is bigger than a single person and it has morphed over time. This is just a little background to let
you see where publishing has been and where it could go. There are no
boundaries on where publishing may go.

Same as Paper, Only Different

It is important to remember that most of the presentation methods used
in the printed format also work well for electronic formats. The borders, boundaries, columns, and rules for good graphics still apply.
There are differences because the computer screen is scanned and read
differently than the printed page. This is shown in the graphics below.

Further, you need to keep the paper in mind if the work that is being
created will ever be printed. On some web sites, you have probably
noticed that there may be a button or an icon that may be used for
printing that item or page. That means that the web page or other

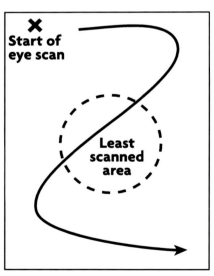

Eye scan of printed single page layout

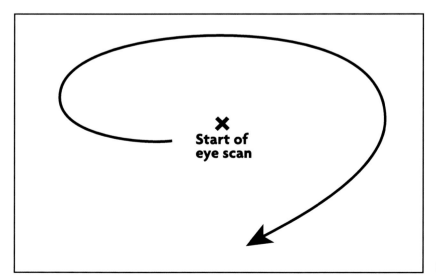

Eye scan of computer monitor

information will be reformatted for optimal printing, not optimal viewing on a monitor.

The point is that the exact format of the content depends on the chosen delivery system. The two primary groups are: web design for stand-alone applications, Internet, or intranet use and eBooks. Both have their own standards. The web style design is much looser and freeform. eBook methods are more rigid, because the technology to view eBooks is more proprietary. There is one catch: the eBook data must be able to be read by any brand of reader. The web style runs on systems that are more open. This section of the chapter will focus on web design.

There are three simple things to remember:

a) Keep your work simple; just as in a small magazine ad, less is more. Keep it clean by removing all clutter. Do not use filler or items just to take up space. Never add something just because you can or technology allows. Write your text with concise wording and keep it brief. Use bullet points.

b) Keep it consistent, have a common theme on similar or related pages. That is, have a standard menu and some background or color that is a common thread to help the user know that the pages are all related.

c) Keep the content relevant, informative, and helpful. Most professional sites should stay away from "cute" animations, songs playing in the background, etc. It does depend on the topic of the site. In any event, keep it professional and minimal to clarify the point of the site to the visitor. All the animated GIF files and WAV or MP3 files take time to load and they may add clutter. Professionally, time is money. Personally, I spend about two hours per day on the Internet doing research. If I have to wait for a site to load, I will go to a different site to try to find the information I need. It comes to a balance; if your client wants a theme song or an animated GIF, keep them as small as possible. Avoid splash screens. If you have to put in an option to "SKIP INTRO," you probably should not have the intro! Some search engines will not list your site if it has a splash screen. You may not be doing your client any favors by putting in the extras!

Books to read:
Designing and Writing Online Documentation by William K. Horton,
Standards for Online Communication by Joann T. Hackos.

Standards of User Interface (HMI)

Unfortunately, there is not a definitive guide to the standards of Human Machine Interface (HMI). There are some guidelines that can help. Mostly, I would call it "common sense." For instance, if you are creating a site that will be primarily directed at people that speak English, the site should read from left to right and top to bottom. Computer programs and the Internet have made some practices common; I personally would refrain from calling them standards. The header should go on the top of the page and menu selections are predominantly on the left side of the screen or at the bottom of the header. People who search an English language web site do not look at the right side of the screen first. They generally will start their eye scan in the center of the monitor and spiral out in a clockwise manner, exiting on the bottom of the screen. As an aside, this is also true in the design of HMI control screens for the operation of equipment and facili-

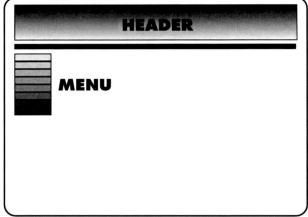

ties. The international flow for the development of these control screens is from top to bottom and from left to right. Then the common practice is to focus on the hierarchy, navigability (ease of browsing), and the flow of information. Study computer programs in general and I think you will understand. This topic goes much deeper than can be addressed in this chapter or even this book. There are several books that you can refer to should you want to get into the subject deeper.

It is best to start with a site map sketch, a story board, design brief or a scope of work document when you are working for a client or even on your own project. This document will help you define the content of your design. In general terms, this document would have a statement that defines the purpose of what you are creating with a statement of expectations. This involves the client and sometimes you have to mine the information out of them. The client needs to write the brief; you may help them out or just ask the questions that need to be answered. Another possible solution is to start with a problem statement to determine the root cause of a problem. The key to this method is to stay away from "solving" the problem. The purpose is to find the "real" or root problem, then find the solution to that problem. This method of problem solving helps to determine root causes. This gets into system analysis and other deeper subjects. If you find yourself getting into this area and would like to know more, read Managing Software Requirements, A Unified Approach by Dean Leffingwell & Don Widrig. Refer to Jakob Nielsen's 10 usability heuristics (using a problem-solving technique to find the best solution from several possible solutions).

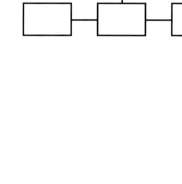

Keep the web site easy to surf, with consistent interface on all pages. For examples, look at and study good professional computer programs and other good web sites. When you build a web site, keep in mind that you are delivering the content in a smaller readable area than printed matter. Further, keep in mind that this information (data) has to be downloaded from a server and across phone lines and a modem that may only be running at 26 Kbps. Maintain fast load times on your site so that the user does not get frustrated and leave. You are building the web site to express, not impress. Web sites to review and study include: www.pcmag.com, www.cnn.com, www.amazon.com, www.time.gov, etc.

Pictures and graphics are worth a thousand words, make each one count. The larger the graphic element is the larger the file is. That means that you need each graphic to only be large enough to be clear. Any larger than it needs to be and it will take longer to load. Microsoft FrontPage allows you to change the size of the image then to click on the resample button. Resampling the graphic removes unnecessary pixels and reduces the file size. In a web site application, the graphic element remains a separate file that is "called" into the web page when the web page is downloaded to be viewed. When you insert a graphic element into a word processing or page layout program, that file will increase in size as the graphic element becomes part of that file. The amount of increase in file size depends on the program and the compression scheme that it uses.

When you build a web site, put phone numbers and addresses on them. One of my peeves is sites without any real contact information: no phone, fax, or mailing address. If you are so ashamed of the site that you do not want to be accountable for it, you probably should not do the work in the first place. I have visited countless business web sites that do not have a singe phone number or mailing address. In cases where I want their information, I go to www.arin.net or www.networkso-lutions.com and look them up by their URL.

While talking about peeves... Never build a site that you will not let the user use the browser's back button! When I cannot use the back button, I vow never to return to that site. It is a method used to trap users into not leaving. While I am doing a search, I may click on a site that will not let me use the back button to return to my search. This has cost me time and caused me frustration. I have even contacted the company to let them know that I think that it is unprofessional to use this technique.

Make links to other sites open in a new window, unless you are ready for them to leave your site. Here are a couple of cases to consider:

When you do NOT want the surfer to leave your site:
Let's say that you are building a site for the investigation of interplane-tary travel and you have a lot to say about your own research and most importantly, you want to sell T-shirts to your visitors. Everyone needs one more logo T-shirt! But... There is this other great site that has addi-tional information or files on it that you think is relevant. First, you get permission to make the link (ask if they would like to link to your site) from the webmaster. Second, you make your link open in a new win-dow. This causes the surfer to come back to you when they close the window on the linked site. They can still buy your awesome logo t-shirt or they can leave on their own. You did not force them to leave.

When you DO want the surfer to leave your site (for a higher purpose of course):
Let's say that you are building a site that sells brass beads. Your client wants to make beads and not deal with the public at large, so they have a dealer network. They want customers to make their purchases from an authorized dealer. When the surfer clicks the buy now button, they end up on a page full of dealer links. They can pick one, click the link and be transported to the dealer's web site to buy.

Introduction to the Internet

I have attempted to keep the first part of this section as brief as possible; it is my way to keep you from going to sleep while reading this. There are some important names and acronyms that you need to know if you are going to dive into the Internet abyss.

The Internet Corporation for Assigned Names and Numbers (ICANN) basically governs the Internet. Only ICANN-accredited domain name registrars are legally allowed to register domain names (ex. www.graph-icdesignpolice.com).

ICANN

The InterNIC was originally developed by several companies in cooperation with the U.S. Government. They are an integrated network information center; they collect and store information relevant to the Internet and its users. InterNIC is a registered service mark of the U.S. Department of Commerce. It is licensed to ICANN.

InterNIC

American Registry for Internet Number (ARIN). ARIN, a nonprofit corporation, allocates Internet Protocol resources.

ARIN

Internet Assigned Numbers Authority (IANA). They deal with Internet Protocol (IP) numbers.

IANA

Registrars are companies that applied to ICANN for the right to sell domain names. They have to fill out an application and be approved before being authorized to sell domain names.

Registrars

Internet Service Provider (ISP) is the company that you connect to for access to the Internet.

ISP

A Uniform Resource Locator (URL) is a page's address; this is the www.whatever.com that is actually the word form of the IP address called a dotted decimal notation (ex. 201.103.61.122).

URL

An intranet is a web site or file repository that can be accessed on ANY closed, private network. You can have an intranet on any two computers that are connected via a network.

intranet

A good practice for building web sites, hypertext document, and other eDocuments is to build them and test them till you are confident that they appear the way you want them to. Now you can publish your site to an intranet to share for real user testing in a multi-user environment or you can publish it to a CD ROM and let individuals test it for you. Practice is good, feedback from critics is priceless, take it all to heart.

At some point you are going to meet, talk to, or at least be introduced to the much feared and revered "Client". The Client is the person that is paying your way and possibly the way of some of the folks that work with you. The Client is king and the Client is ALWAYS right... Well maybe in some sense that is true. However, even today with dot coms failing every single day, some Clients will probably always think that the Internet is filled with gold just waiting to be mined. Be polite, be tactful, be professional, and be honest. The Internet is a dangerous place where you can lose the contents of your wallet faster than you can say "web-master." Don't waste your client's money, in the form of time or boondoggles or things you know will not work or will not help them with the objective of their electronic publication that you are working on.

The following is just my opinion; I know that it is shared by many people, though. Time is not a renewable resource and it just should not be wasted on bad web sites that do not work and do not serve some purpose other than to eat up the bandwidth for others. Take a look at a great web site to get a feel for what I am telling you. Go to www.websitesthatsuck.com. I would rather not find out that someone that read this book went and designed a web site for dancing chipmunks. Here are some thoughts on some types of web sites that are helpful and desirable:

-News
-Information
-Sales
-Research
-File delivery

Most other web sites are a waste of hard disk space and bandwidth!

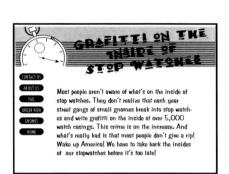

More on technology: plug-ins for browsers are commonly required. I recommend that you build your sites for the Internet without the requirement to go and get a plug-in just so the user can look at your site. When I run into sites that have an introduction or require a plug-in just to browse, I move on instantly. For some folks, the Internet is entertainment, just like TV, only interactive and they have all the time they want, or it is a hobby, or they have unlimited hard disk space on their computer. For whatever reason, some people will load anything that is FREE on to their computer. Most professionals will not. They want to know the value, the resources, and the cost in terms of bandwidth or disk space. If you must have a plug-in, make it so that is available to the user on that page at least in the form of a link (ex. Acrobat). Make sure that the plug-in link opens a new window so that when the user is done with the plug-in install, they do not have to find your site again. It is still there waiting and ready for them to continue.

The use of frames in online documents does not seem to be growing. Frames, like plug-ins, can be good and bad. According to the statistics I have seen on the Internet, most people are using browsers that do not view frames properly. Further, most of the folks out there in Internet land are running at a 800 X 600 resolution on Windows '95/'98 computers.

Keep your sites updated and fresh every few months. It keeps people coming back and it lets them know that you care enough about the site and them to keep them informed and that you continue to strive for quality.

All eDocuments must run on different platforms. That means that the documents you create will need to be read on computers that are Windows, Mac OS, UNIX, Linux, Sun Solaris, and all the rest (there are a vast quantity of operating systems). So your documents must be in a standard format that can be read and understood by all these operating systems. Some of the most common file types are .htm, .html, .gif, .jpg, .pdf, .tif, .txt, .wav, and .zip. There are many others.

On-line information, documents, and brochures are terrific ways to share information rapidly and, hopefully, clearly and fully. These types of documents can be full sites, pages, or specific files. Access can be full and without any security or you can secure the site, page, or file with a user-name and / or password. For the sake of conversation, let's say that you have a web site that you are creating that you want visitors to be able to download or view free sample pages of a book. This would be a case that you would not want to use any level of security, because you do not want to restrict access. In a different scenario, let's say that you have a web page where a business partner needs access to information that you post in a specific file everyday and the business partner is the only person that should have access to the file. Instead of just posting this link on a public site, you may build a secure site just for your interactions or possibly create a site where only a portion of it is secure. Another option may be to put the file in a directory where it resides without any connection to any web site. You can then just email the link to the business partner and secure the file so that the file cannot be accessed without a user name and password. Once the file is accessed, you can determine if you want the file to be opened, downloaded, printed, or whatever. Some files like .pdf can be internally secured even further (examples include: limiting access, authoring, extracting, printing, etc.). Just remember this: there is no such thing as a totally secure eDocument. If it can be seen on a screen or printed, it can be captured and put into a different format. All of these scenarios can be played out on the Internet or on any intranet. It can also apply to documents stored in any media type.

CD ROM or any digital media format can be used for the storage and access of eDocuments and information, just like on the Internet. In order to secure the disk and add other refinements to the "front end" of the data or information you are including on the disk, you will have to learn about programming and/or hire a programmer. It is not my intent to cover this subject any further than this. To learn more, go to the library or the Internet.

Get Found on the Web

Before you start on your web design project, it is important to know how people will find your new site. It is staggering to realize the quantity of new sites being published to the web everyday. Your new site will be only one in a sea of thousands. Besides the advertising, links from other sites, brochures, and word of mouth, search engines are the way your site will get visitors. Here are some things to consider. Each page of your site needs to have the words that make your site unique repeated. If you have key words that you think will be used to find your site, use those key words consistently. Search engines are just large databases and they catalog sites according to content, page titles, and the meta names keywords section at the top of the index.htm page. The index.htm page is the first page that comes up on any web site. If you are building a site for a company that wants to sell big red ships, the scenario would go something like this:

a. A good domain name would be www.bigredships.com.

b. The keywords at the top of the index.htm page would be something like <META NAME="keywords" CONTENT="big red ships, ocean ships, ships, red ships, big ships, shipping, vessels">

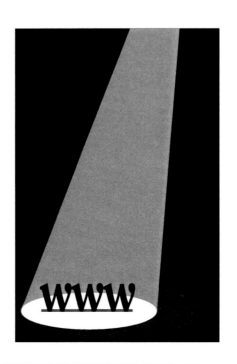

c. The body of the page would state something like: Big Red Ships sells ships around the world. Big Red Ships manufactures the world's largest ocean going shipping vessels and ships. We at Big Red Ships are proud of our ships. We have been building the best ocean going ships since 1492...

The point is not really to be blatant about the word usage; however, the more times a word shows up, the higher the site will be in the search ranking.

So, what are the mechanics of getting listed on a search engine? Well, sad to say, most search engines will not list your site for free. There are still some sites that will. For the free search engines, you usually have to dig into their sites and find a link that is something like "list your site", "recommend a site", etc. Then you just answer the questions. It is not hard, it just takes time and it can take months to get your site listed on a search engine. There are companies that will list your site with thousands of search engines for a fee. You pay the fee and they do all the work. The choice is yours. Make sure that your site is search engine friendly. I recommend reading all the information available on each search engine site for the rules that apply. They can be sticky about it and they can make it so that your site will never get listed for certain types of infringements to their rules. Most are reasonable and even desirable for keeping the web a place people want to be.

Anyone Can Publish a Website

So you are about ready to get a web site rolling. You will need a place for this site to be published to. That is, you will need a web host. A web host is a company that has access to the Internet with some fast servers and lots of hard disk space. Companies range from hosting sites for free to charging way too much. Hosting services can include things like web statistics, ecommerce solutions (like shopping carts), email addresses, etc. You want to look for a web host that will serve your needs now and into the future. The highlight for selecting a web host is this: value. You will have to make the final determination for yourself. To me, value in web hosting is found in up-time, control and ownership of my information (setting up my own emails, passwords, etc.), security options, able to publish my stuff my way (even if it is in FrontPage or File Transfer Protocol (FTP)), speed, and the true cost per year (in terms of time and money). That is to say that if my web site is not running, it is not doing anything for me or anyone else. It is useless. It has zero value and if I am paying any amount of money, it is too much.

My advice is to not do a free web hosting service as FREE usually has its own price. Find a company that has been doing it for some time (I suggest at least 3 years), who are on a major telephone backbone, who let you set up domains and manage the site for yourself and/or your clients, who do not share any of your information with anyone, and who let you set up your own email accounts. Avoid any web host that has canned web stuff (templates) that you have to use, any web host that says "...fast, easy, no html, choose from 110 award winning web site designs". Avoid any host that will not let you log in to a site using FTP or any other method you need for managing your site and files. I know that I am leaving a lot out on this topic. There are just too many companies and too many variables. You will have to do the research. Look on the web and search for "web host ratings" and "web hosting".

To publish a web site there are a few things you will need and there are many options. You can learn about html, java, perl, xml, and other web technologies and write code and programs from scratch using a text editor. Then you can get a program to upload your files to the remote site, using FTP. Some folks would say that this is the only correct way to build web sites. Well, I will tell you that there are several programs that you design in and it will convert the design into HTML for you. You then tell the program you are ready to publish and it will publish and manage changes for you. You can do the html if you choose to, you just do not have to. You can use programs like FrontPage by Microsoft, Dreamweaver by macromedia and freeware from all kinds of people. These HTML WYSIWYG (What You See Is What You Get) editors allow you to see what it looks like in a browser or edit the file in HTML mode. Purists do not care for them because it removes the mystique of programming. It does not bother me if I cannot follow all the HTML code in my site. What I care about is: does the site look good, does it work correctly, and does it load fast.

Now with all that said, most of the best sites in the world are developed with love and care by professional programmers and graphic designers. Programmers and graphic designers work together to come up with the best sites on the web. In addition, the best sites are tested by professional users and novice users alike. Some of the sites are even reviewed by what marketing folks call "focus groups." A focus group is a group of folks that is selected to tell what they think about a specific site, product, movie, political idea, etc. If you want to learn to do graphic design and be a programmer, you will probably always have a job.

So, what is FTP and what does it mean to me? FTP allows you to login to a remote computer or site and manage the files at that location remotely. The FTP program may integrate seamlessly into your current file management tool or it may look completely different. The outcome is the same. You are able to see the file structure and the files that they contain. Further, you may use it to move, delete, or copy files at that location or upload and download files. FTP sites can be helpful when working with large files that will not fit on to a digital memory device or media or you do not want to mail it. The way this works is you log into an FTP site, you upload the files you want to share, and there they sit. Most FTP sites will send an email notification to whomever you choose. The purpose of this notification is to alert the person you are sharing files with that the files are at the FTP site and are ready for them to download. FTP programs are available for little money or even free.

HTML –
Not Just for Web Publishing

This is not a programmer's guide; there are literally thousands of books on programming. You do not have to be a programmer to build strong web sites or to build on-line documentation. In fact, I think that the way a site is presented and interacted with is far more important than perfect code. Use your design skills to focus on the user interface and sharing the information of the site with the folks that come to visit.

Remember that the purpose of your design is to express, not impress. So use any tool that works for you. I have used Microsoft products for years. Not because I thought they were the best, but the tools are adequate and readily available with tons of documentation and information about them. Please note that this is NOT an endorsement of Microsoft or Microsoft products. In producing web sites, I have used: FrontPage, Publisher, & even Word. The first web site I produced was created in Publisher. It was not a great site; however, it worked. As I learned more about the limitations of Publisher, I moved up to FrontPage. It was part of the Microsoft suite that I purchased and I still use it today to create, manage, and edit my web site (www.sixbranches.com) and the web sites of others. I have even used Word to produce a quick site that I used as a re-direction page. In Word, you can simply save your work as HTML. Then I used FTP to publish the single page.

There are literally hundreds of programs out there that will fill the need that you have. The trick is to find one that YOU can use and meets your needs.

Dot Bombs are not the End of Internet Business

The Internet Gold Rush is over; the Internet is not dead, merely beginning to mature. The Dot Com collapse is over. Now Dot Coms are not any different from any other starting company. Most will fail. Internet businesses failing have helped add to the economic and stock market down turn that has been experienced in 2001-2002. There were more millionaires made in the 1990's than any other time. Dot Com businesses had only to fire up a server and get on the Web to make their millions. The stocks were massively over valued and have since corrected themselves. That is what I call the Internet gold rush. Like any new toy or business, the glamour wears thin and you are left with the grind, not the glitz. Every industry does this boom, bust, and stabilization. In any event, the Internet is simply out of the gold rush stage and is maturing to become a tool that is invaluable for information and research. The days of an HTML programmer earning more than the company president are probably over. There will always be room for great designers and programmers to create eDocuments of all types. Just know that you may have to wear both hats!

Final Internet thoughts

The darker side of the Internet is real. There are people from every country looking to make a profit on you and from your interactions with the Internet. It may be as simple as selling your personal information, legal or not. Marketing people and governments keep looking for ways to get everyone on the Internet. Yet, here in the USA, arguably the richest nation in the world, we still have people without running water, power, or telephones in their houses. There are many areas in the USA that do not have touch-tone or digital dialing. More importantly, there are many Americans giving up all types of technology to help keep their lives simple.

Send Emails That Have Links To Large Files That You Do Not Want To Email

Here are a couple of thoughts about email and eDocuments. eDocuments can become large fast. I personally become uneasy about sending emails that are over one megabyte. However, in the type of work I do, I have sent files that are up to four megabytes. A consideration is to upload the file you need someone to view and even print to an Internet server and just email the link or URL for that file. I have in some cases emailed a rather large .PDF file that contained hyperlinks to other even larger files that are sitting on my server. I would further say that there is no wrong or right way; these are just some thoughts that needed to be shared. After all, email and hyperlinks are basic eDocuments.

Abuse of email and computers is at an all time high. A part of this is simply because more people than ever before have access to powerful computing systems and fast telecommunications on a global scale. HTML is used for emails as well. Email may also contain java elements, animated .gif files, and other time wasting, sometimes amusing, antics. Emails can also contain viruses, worms, and hyperlinks. Emails may not include a virus, worm, or data that you can see. However, elements in an email file can download data and files from other servers on to your computer. The people that mail spam have also created email files so that when you open email, it just validates your email address on their server so they can sell your email address. Further, there are many type of Trojan horse-type of emails. The mail may come to you in the form of an electronic greeting card, from a friend. It will probably include a link; once the link is activated, the program that you did not want to launch, does. It can deliver a file to you, it can download your address book, or perform any number of nefarious deeds. The link you click may also tell you that you need a plug-in to view the greeting card, then do the same thing.

Computer Graphics Explained:

Computer graphics come in two fundamentally different formats. These formats are called bitmap and vector graphics.

Bitmap graphics are sometimes referred to as raster graphics. Bitmaps are rows and columns of dots (pixels). The number of dots you can manipulate is directly related to the resolution of the monitor you are working on, 800 X 600 Dots Per Inch (DPI) is common. Bitmap images are created using "paint" programs. The way this works is, you can turn each pixel on and off. When you turn it on, you can set the color for each dot. When bitmap images are enlarged or scaled up, they begin to look rough and jagged; they can be scaled down in most cases and still be usable. Fax machines, digital copy machines, scanners, and other similar technology convert analog or vector graphics into a bitmap. That is why the scanning resolution of a scanner is critical. When you have an existing image that must be scanned, the resolution of the graphic becomes important. If the scan must be smooth looking, the scan resolution must be higher than 600 dpi. It is important to

The two photo examples below show how pixels make a bitmap image out of a photograph. Usually, the resolution is high enough (which means the number of pixels per inch is high enough) that the human eye can't detect them. Normally the pictures below would look smooth, but we have exaggerated the pixels by making the resolution low so that you could see how rough and jagged a photo looks when it is in low resolution. It reminds you of needlepoint. It's called "pixilation."

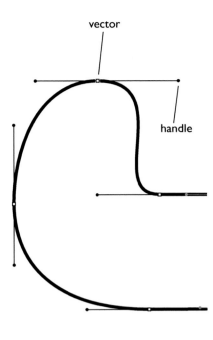

vector

handle

remember that the higher the resolution (more dots per inch) the larger the file becomes. Bitmap file size can change dramatically because of physical size and resolution.

Vector graphics, also called object-oriented graphics, are made up of objects (lines, arcs, circles, text). These objects are defined as vectors. That is, the lines, arc, circles, and text are all defined mathematically and are stored as formulas in the program's database. Every graphic item is an object. A vector is a line with a start point, an angle (a direction) and magnitude (distance). Vector graphics can be created in Computer Aided Drafting (CAD) programs and in "draw" programs. Vector graphics store more intelligence with the graphic and the file size is generally smaller and more dimensionally accurate than bitmaps. Vector graphics can be scaled up and down because mathematical formulas define the objects; they are not defined as dots. Vector graphics are best created and not scanned. A good technique to convert scanned images to a vector graphic is to import the scanned image, then trace over it using a vector graphic program.

Scanning technology can convert raster graphics to vector graphics. This can take time and it does not always work; all scanned images will have to be checked for accuracy. The reason for this is that the scanner sees every dot on the page, then the software used with the scanner interprets the each dot to determine if it is valid or not. Sometimes the software makes the wrong choices and creates errors. Some cases where this type of technology is used are in converting drawings to CAD format used in engineering and illustrating for storage and editing. A second use is Optical Character Recognition (OCR) used to convert existing text into a file that can be edited with a computer.

About Copyrights

Become familiar with copyright procedures and requirements. There is the standard copyright for printed material, the Digital Millennium Copyright Act (DMCA), and copyrights for recorded materials. It is in your best interest to become familiar with this aspect of graphics. A good place to start is http://www.loc.gov/copyright/

Final Note

Even as this book is being printed, some of the information is becoming outdated. Keep up to date on current technology changes. Read technical journals. Visit www.techweb.com, www.redhat.com, www.microsoft.com, www.adobe.com, etc. Cyber space is changing rapidly and the pace is tough; however, the effort will pay off.

On May 9, 2001, after being the subject of a daring pursuit across 7 continents by the Graphic Design Police, the notorious Narilla Hespariddle was captured at the top of a ferris wheel in an amusement park in Wales. 781 people had almost died after they saw Hespariddle's website for "Grafitti on the Inside of Stop Watches." It wasn't so much the subject of the website that made all those people swoon – although "Poetry on the Inside of Pocket Watches" would have been a more tasteful choice – rather it was the 3 graphic design felonies she committed in the design of the front page to the website.

Narilla Hespariddle

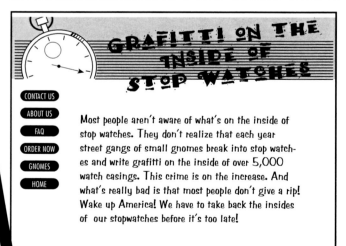

This space represents part of the web page the viewer scrolls down through

EXHIBIT A:

1. As you can see, Hespariddle's web design has a black background. This is a no-no because if people want to print out the information, they'll end up using up all the ink or toner in their printer and take a long time doing it.

2. Hespariddle's next felony is the text that is justified to the right. Type that is set this way is hard to read, especially on a computer screen on a black background.

3. And there is no sign of any hyperlink buttons until you scan waaaay down to the bottom of the page. The viewer shouldn't have to hunt for things that should be obvious.

It's bad news all over for the web page viewer, so chances are you'll chase him or her away real fast.

EXHIBIT B:
After Narilla served her sentence in a clock factory and was thunked in the head a few times by the judge throwing the book at her, she went back and redesigned the web page so it was more efficient.

Now the page has a nice simple, white background like most professional websites have, and the type is justified to the left for easier reading. Also, the buttons are in plain sight so the viewer doesn't have to search for them.

Important Things To Remember

1. *What is electronic publishing?*

2. *What is HTML?*

3. *What is an eBook?*

4. *Do people scan computer screens the same way they read books?*

5. *What is HMI?*

6. *What is the Internet?*

7. *What is an intranet?*

8. *What is a web host?*

9. *Where would I find a web host?*

10. *What is the best way to find other sites on the Internet?*

11. *What is a bitmap graphic?*

12. *What is a vector graphic?*

13. *What does WYSIWYG stand for?*

14. *What does FTP stand for?*

15. *Where do you go to register copyrights in the United States?*

16. *What is a zip file?*

17. *What is a good technical resource?*

18. *What is a computer platform?*

19. *Who invented the Internet?*

20. *What is your favorite color?*

Answers on page 144

Answers

1. *Electronic publishing is the distribution of any document or art in electronic format or digital media.*

2. *HTML is a programming tool used for the Internet and other documents.*

3. *An eBook is a blend of hardware and software used to create interactive books.*

4. *No. People do not scan computer screens the same way they read books.*

5. *HMI stands for Human Machine Interface.*

6. *The Internet is a global network of personal, corporate, and government computers that has both public and private access areas.*

7. *An intranet is a web site that can exist on any private network or computer.*

8. *A web host is a company that rents hard disk space on servers and virtual servers for web and FTP sites.*

9. *You can find a web host on the Internet.*

10. *The best way to find other sites on the Internet is to use a search engine.*

11. *A bitmap graphic is created by a "paint" program and is pixel oriented. The color of each pixel can be controlled.*

12. *A vector graphic is created by a "drawing" program and is vector oriented. The color, size, and direction of each element may be controlled by tiny electronic points called handles to control or modify the vectors of elements in some applications.*

13. *WYSIWYG stands for What You See Is What You Get.*

14. *FTP stands for File Transfer Protocol.*

15. *You go to the U.S. Copyright Office to register copyrights in the United States.*

16. *A zip file may contain one or more files. These files are compressed to take up less space.*

17. *A good technical resource for computer information is www.techweb.com.*

18. *A computer platform consists of CPU and OS.*

19. *No one person invented the Internet. It is the result of the spontaneous combustion of ideas.*

20. *Everyone needs to have a favorite color.*

Abstract: In drawing or painting, real things are still recognizable but have been distorted or stylized for a certain effect. In graphic design, "abstract" can be applied to shapes and means a mix of geometric and freeform shapes to simplify real things into graphic symbols such as in logo design.

Alignment: The arrangement of graphic object and/or type in a straight line vertically or horizontally. Alignment can be done either along the sides of objects or type or by aligning the object or type itself along its horizontal or vertical center axis.

All Caps: a characteristic of type which is short for "All Capital Letters" where no lower case letters are used.

Ascender: The stroke of a lowercase letter that extends above the lowercase height of the letter "x." Lowercase letters that have ascenders are b, d, f, h, k, l, t.

ASCII: Acronym for the American Standard Code for Information Interchange. Pronounced ask-ee, ASCII represents English characters as numbers, with each letter assigned a number from 0 to 127. For example, ASCII code for uppercase A is 66. ASCII text is plain, unformatted text. No bolding, no underlines, etc.

Asymmetry: In a layout or composition a type of balance that is not symmetrical. In symmetrical balance all the elements are centered or have a mirror image effect with the vertical axis at the center. In asymmetrical balance all the elements are off-centered but still balanced by weight distribution and alignment.

Background: One type of graphic object that can be used as a design element on a page. Backgrounds usually cover the whole page like wallpaper or wrapping paper designs and have pictures and type placed over them.

Balance: One of the design rules or principles of design. Balance is an equal distribution of weight in a layout. Symmetry and asymmetry are two types of balance. Alignment is also a very important aspect of balance.

Bandwidth: Represents the amount of data that can be transmitted during any given amount of time. This is usually measured in Bits per Second (bps). This is important for I/O devices (anything that communicates electronically, digitally or analog).

Baseline: The invisible line on which type sits.

Bitmap: Raster graphic. Turn each pixel on or off and set a color. Used in paint programs.

Block Of Type: Any area of body text such as one or two paragraphs or a column of text.

Body Type: Also called "Body Text," and "Body Copy," this is the main text of an article or story that is made very easy to read by being typeset in a font that does not call attention to itself, but instead lets the reader concentrate on the content of what is being said in the article.

Border: A design, line or decorative element on the edge or rim of the page or on the edge of a certain area of the page. Most borders are rectangular in nature.

Box: Usually a rectangle with a border of some sort. Type and other graphic objects are put into a box to make sidebars, cartoons, etc.

Bullet: A small round black circle that is "x" height size that is usually put at the beginning of each item in a list. Bullets can vary in design, some being diamonds, squares, flowers, stars, etc.

CAD: Computer Aided Drafting program. Used for design, drafting, and illustrations. Uses vector graphics.

Caption: The descriptive text underneath a photo or an illustration. This type is usually set in a size and style of type that contrasts with the body copy of the article. Sometimes it is bold and/or italic.

Cartoon: A simple illustration that exaggerates and makes its subjects abstract in such a humorous way so as to evoke laughter from the reader.

Cartouche: A small mini-design usually a curly-cue, leaf design or flourish that is used to take up space between blocks of copy and for other design purposes.

Casual Type: A category of type that looks hand drawn, informal, exaggerated and wild.

Clip Art and Symbol fonts: These fonts are simply graphic objects that have been turned into font format.

CMYK Color: Process color for printing is composed of four ink colors: Cyan, Magenta, Yellow, and Black; CMYK for short. Halftone screens in each color are composed of tiny dots which, depending on their size and proximity to each other, determine how light or dark a color will be. So, by mixing varying halftone percentages of Cyan, Magenta, Yellow, and Black you can achieve every color in the rainbow on the printing press.

Color: One of the tools or elements of design. This tool is one of the best at attracting the viewer's eye to your design. Things can be printed in black and white, mechanical colors or full color.

You can create moods and emotion with color; organize your layout using color; use color to help identify things either literally or symbolically.

Column: A column of type is made up of many paragraphs which, when put together, make a long vertical block of type. A page can be divided into 1, 2, 3, 4, or 5 columns of type that are side by side, depending on the width of the page. Columns are vertical. Rows are horizontal.

Common File types: .gif — graphics interchange format, .htm — hyper text markup language, dot 3 format, .html — hyper text markup language, .jpg — Joint Photographic Experts Group, format for color images, .mp3 — Moving Picture Experts Group, MPEG audio layer 3, .pdf - Portable Document Format, developed by Adobe Systems, .tif — tagged image file format, .txt - ASCII text, .wav - Standard sound file, developed by IBM & Microsoft, .zip - data compression format. Used to compress one or more files into one file. Can also be an .exe to be a self-extracting file.

Compression: See Data

Conflict: This is what happens when you are trying to use the design rule of contrast, but don't quite achieve it. If you are trying to contrast type in style and size and you make your two samples only slightly different, it almost looks like a typesetting mistake, and hence, a conflict. When you have conflict in your layout, not only does the whole design look like a mistake, but it also looks timid and uncertain.

Contrast: One of the design rules or principles of design. Elements of a layout look like they don't belong together because they are vastly different from each other.

Crop: To choose a certain area of a photo or illustration for reproduction and cut away the rest as unnecessary.

Crosshatching: A method of shading in pen and ink illustration where parallel lines are drawn in one direction, and then parallel lines are drawn in a perpendicular direction over the first set of lines.

Cut And Paste: A term used in page layout and draw software to describe the process of deleting an object or type from one page or document and placing it onto another page or document.

Data Compression: Compressed data files store data more efficiently, thereby requiring less space. Data compression is used extensively in data transmissions and for archival purposes. The data is compressed using different data compression algorithms. Popular data compression types are .ARC (developed by Systems Enhancement Associates) and .ZIP (developed by Phil Katz and offered by many companies). The ZIP format can also have an .EXE extension as it can be a self-extracting archive.

Depth: The vertical measurement of any part of your layout.

Descender: The stroke of a lowercase letter that extends below the the lowercase height of the letter "x." Lowercase letters that have descenders are g, j, p, q, y.

Design brief: A document that is usually written by the client that states all the criteria that needs to be met for any project. Can also be called a specification.

Diagonal: Anything that has a slanted or oblique direction in relationship to the vertical or horizontal.

Diagram: A sketch, drawing, chart or graph, not necessarily representational, designed to demonstrate or explain something.

Digital Media: This includes any media that can store data for extended periods of time for retrieval at a later time. This includes any type of disk, tape, or memory system: magnetic, laser, or hardware.

Dingbat: A type element or mini-design used to create a border, a bullet or some other design element in your layout.

Display Type: Also called Headline Type, this category of type sets the tone or evokes the feeling of the article or whatever you are trying to convey by calling attention to itself by means of it's unique design. This type is unlike Body Copy where subtle, low key letterforms are used.

Dominance: One of the design rules or principles of design. With dominance you must have a hierarchy of importance to all the elements of your layout. One element has to be the most important and one has to be the least important with all the other elements in between – one being a little more important than the other.

Dot Gain: Grays are produced by printing Black halftone dots of different sizes. In offset printing there are problems maintaining the open spaces between those dots, especially with the darker tones from 60-90%, because the dots are so big and the spaces between the dots are so tiny. So the dots can clog up. It's easier to keep the spaces between the dots open in the lighter values of gray such as 20, 30 and 50%.

Download: Downloading is the act of copying a file from a remote or connected computer to the computer that you are using. Also see Upload.

Double Truck: Two pages in a book, magazine or newspaper which face each other when the publication is opened. Usually a double truck has one ad or one article laid out on it. Also known as a two-page spread.

eBook: eBooks are books that have been written or converted to a software standard that allows it to be used in an eBook reader or related hardware device.

ePublishing: Publishing any work on a media that can be retrieved using digital hardware or software.

Feathering: A term used to describe the process of softening the edge of a photo in a program such as PhotoShop.

Fill And Stroke: In a draw program, all shapes can be "filled" with a color or pattern and their edges can also be defined by a colored line or "stroked."

Focal Point: A good layout has a focal point where the eye is drawn first above all other places in the composition. The focal point is usually the dominant or emphasized element in your layout. This is usually created when one element differs from the rest in size, color, line, texture, or etc.

Font: See Typeface.

Footer: Reoccurring chapter names and numbers, name of book, page numbers, or etc. that are positioned at the bottom of each page of a magazine, newspaper, newsletter or book. Many times there is a line (or rule) over the type in a footer.

Freeform: Irregular shapes like silhouettes of people, animals, plants or just non-objective shapes that look like they have been drawn quickly by hand or made by accident.

FTP: File Transfer Protocol. Used to upload and download files to or from a server.

Geometric: Mathematical looking and precise shapes like circles, squares, triangles, diamonds, rectangles and octagons.

Gradation: One of the design rules or principles of design. Gradation is a gradual change of any design tool in a composition and provides a smooth transition between areas of the design. Feathered edges on photos, airbrushed gradient backgrounds going from dark to light or from a warm color to a cool color are the most obvious examples.

Gradient: Usually a background area that gradually and smoothly changes from a dark value or color to a lighter value or color. The effect is like an airbrush painted the background.

Graphic Object: Any kind of a visual picture or design other than the body copy on the page. Graphic objects consist of rules; borders; boxes, panels, shapes; clip art and illustrations; photos; cartouches and dingbats; logos; pull quotes and backgrounds.

Grayscale: Usually applied to photographic images or artwork that have different values of gray areas in them and no color. Distinguished from line art which only has black and white and no gray areas. As far as the human eye can easily discern, there are usually about 10 steps of gray on a grayscale.

Halftone Screen: Different values of grays and colors are produced by printing halftone dots of different sizes and proximity. There are different resolutions of halftone screens. The greater the resolution, the smaller the dots in the screen. The smaller the dots, the clearer and sharper the photo is. Resolution is measured by lines (or dots) per inch or lpi. Common halftone screens are 85, 100, 133, and 150 lpi.

Header: Reoccurring titles, dates, etc. that are the same at the top of each page of a magazine, newspaper, newsletter or book. Many times there is a line (or rule) underneath the type in a header.

Headline Type: The title of an article, blurb or some other piece of writing, usually set in a heavier weight and/or larger size than the body text of the article. This category of type is also known as Display Type.

Heuristics: A way to stimulate a users interest to investigate further.

HMI: Acronym for Human Machine Interface. The interface between human and machine, a control center.

Horizontal: Anything, such as a line, plane or object that is parallel with the horizon. Also movement of anything can be considered horizontal if it moves from left to right or right to left, which is considered parallel with the horizon.

HTML: Hypertext Markup Language. Used for creating documents that can be accessed on the Web.

Hypertext: Hypertext allows a user to jump from place to place in a text or to a URL or to a specific file. In short it is a link. Hypertext was invented in 1975 at Xerox's Palo Alto Research Center (PARC).

Illustration: The category of Illustration is contrasted with that of photography. There are many types of illustration such as cartoons, paintings, pencil drawings, sketchy drawings, technical illustration, loose illustration and tight illustration, realistic and impressionistic illustration. Illustrations are graphic objects used in layouts.

Initial Caps: Refers to capitalizing the first letter of a word.

Internet: This is the World Wide Web and beyond. The Internet is a network of computers that spans the globe with computers that are public, private, and corporate.

Intranet: A web site that is run for private use on a local or wide area network. It is not generally available to people who work outside the organization that it supports. In general, they are private and secure.

IP: Internet Protocol. The IP address is a dotted decimal notation that is actually the number notation for a URL. See URL.

ISP: Internet Service Provider. Any service that allows a computer or other device to be connected to the Internet. These companies are generally connected directly to telecommunication trunk lines via telephone lines or cable. They can provide dial-up or broadband connections.

Issue Number: A number used to designate each issue of a magazine or newsletter. For example, if you have a monthly magazine, there will be twelve issues to the volume. The volume designates the year.

Italics: A characteristic of type where the type leans to the right. This characteristic makes your text look a little like handwriting or calligraphy, lending it a more poetic and artistic nature. It's used mainly for words that need emphasis or for quotations, poems or invitations.

Java: A high-level object-oriented programming language developed by Sun Microsystems

Kbps: Kilobits per second. This is a measure of the amount of data that is being passed through a device, usually in reference to a modem.

Kerning: The space between letters in a line of type. Most people don't realize that the computer doesn't always put accurate spacing between letters and that the typesetter has to kern the letters a little closer together, especially in headlines, to make the typesetting look more professional.

Landscape: A software designation which describes a rectangular box

or page as being in a horizontal position.

Layout: The arrangement, plan or structuring of printed matter as in a magazine or newspaper. A layout can also be called a dummy, mockup, or sketch.

Leading: The space between lines of type, usually measured in points just like type. If the line spacing is to close, the body text becomes cramped and hard to read. Sometimes you can increase the spacing between the lines to create a design effect.

Letterform: The design of a letter which distinguishes it from other type fonts.

Line: One of the tools or elements of design. Lines can be used in pen & ink to shade a drawing. Or they can be as basic as a straight line, also known as a "rule." There are curved lines, dotted lines, fat lines, thin lines, jagged lines, squiggly lines. Lines can be scribbled, crosshatched, sketchy, geometric, directional, horizontal, vertical, or diagonal.

Line Drawing: A black and white drawing composed of lines and black areas having no gray areas or color.

Logo: A simple graphic symbol or design which communicates the identity of a company and/or product to the public. One only has to see the graphic symbol to trigger the image of the company or product in his mind.

Logotype: Similar to a logo in that it serves the same purpose of communicating the identity of a company and/or product to the public, but a logotype usually consists of the words of the name of the company or product that have been made into a graphic design.

Loose: A style of illustration that's sketchy or looks like it's been done quickly or without much effort.

Lower Case: The letters of the alphabet set so that they aren't capital letters.

Margin: The space around the perimeter of the page between the edge of the page and the type in the middle of the page.

Masthead: A long horizontal banner at the top of the first page of a newsletter which has the name of the newsletter, the volume number, the issue number, a slogan, or other descriptive type about the company or the newsletter. Usually mastheads are anywhere from an inch to an inch and a half deep and stretch from the left margin to the right margin.

Mechanical Color: There are different companies that pre-mix Cyan, Magenta, Yellow and Black inks and give them special numbers or names. One of the most well known companies is PANTONE and they have a color structure known as the Pantone Matching System (PMS). Usually PMS colors or other mechanical colors are used in a limited way when you only want Black and one or two other colors.

Medieval and Calligraphy: A form of writing where Scribes from the Medieval period used wedged-shaped pens to write by hand onto parchment, following the serif letter forms of the Romans, and later creating their own interesting letter forms using thicks and thins. Unlike type fonts, calligraphy is unique every time the calligrapher writes it. Modern type fonts in this category mimic the old handwritten style.

Memory Device: Any type of device or media that can store information for an extended period of time

Monitor: Computer screen.

Montage: A style of drawing or painting where many different pictures are arranged closely together or superimposed upon each other into one pictorial composition.

Movement: The illusion of movement can be created in several ways on the printed page. One way is to use the principle of repetition with variation. Another way is to show the sequential frames of an animation action. Or you can show time passing by displaying a series of pictures showing a flower blooming. A fast visual rhythm creates movement by employing sweeping, curving lines or tilting a picture of a train, plane or car. Movement always adds interest to a layout.

Network: Created when two or more computers are connected together. This can include peer-to-peer, server / client, Local Area Networks (LAN), and Wide Area Networks (WAN).

Non-Objective Design: This is what most people describe as "modern art." It is called "non-objective" because *no objects* are pictured. In other words, nothing recognizable that you can put a tag or a name on is depicted in the design, drawing or painting. It is purely art for the sake of the design or the brush strokes, or the lines, or the chalk marks, or etc. Non-objective art is also intriguing because visually-oriented people can find their own objects, landscapes, people, animals, etc. in what they are seeing. This art is good for stimulating the imagination.

OCR: Optical Character Recognition. Used for converting existing documents into a digital format that can be edited.

Operating System (OS): The operating system is the software that makes the processor work. It takes care of passing data to and from the CPU and other hardware for processing.

Out Of Register: A piece of paper has to be run through the printing press 4 times in order to print each of the CMYK colors on top of each other. Each color has to be laid *exactly* on top of the other for everything to look right. If any color is not placed exactly, then it is called "out of register," and it will look like a double or blurred image or you will see small white gaps between areas of color.

Page Grid: An invisible structure of lines which measures out columns and rows on which to align headlines, body copy, and graphic objects. Grids help organize a layout with many visual elements, speed up layout production and contribute to a uniform appearance of a publication.

Panel: Similar to a box, but it can be any geometric shape and can have a border or not. Many times panels are just areas of flat color with type and graphic objects used inside them.

Pantone Color: See Mechanical Color.

Pattern: The rhythm of lights and darks unique to every object or surface, establishes a recognizable texture or pattern. New patterns are created when artists repeat images, designs or type on paper to create backgrounds or borders. Wallpaper or wrapping paper and clothes are common places where you will see pattern.

Perl: Practical Extraction and Report Language. Perl is a programming language developed especially for processing text. Perl is one of the most popular languages for writing CGI scripts.

Photographic Retouching: Sometimes, after a photo has been shot, it has to be further enhanced to achieve the desired effect. It can either be retouched in a subtle way so you can't tell it has been retouched or it can be as exaggerated as putting a dog's head on a man's body. Photos used to be retouched using paint brushes and airbrushes, but nowadays they are retouched using computer software, such as PhotoShop.

Platform: A computing platform is comprised of hardware and an operating system. An example: AMD Athlon CPU running the Linux OS.

Plug-in: A program or driver that is required to run a specific part of a web site. An example is a video may require QuickTime loaded so the video will run.

Portrait: A software designation which describes a rectangular box or page as being in a vertical position.

Positive And Negative Space: The space inside the shape of objects you draw on paper is known as positive space. The space between objects is known as negative space.

Process Color: See CMYK

Proximity: This term is connected to the design tool of space. Realizing that the space around and between objects and type is just as tangible as the objects and type themselves, the most obvious use of this space is the proximity of things to each other on a page. The less space there is between elements – the more proximity – the more they look related.

Pull Quote: A short, interesting, shocking or thought-provoking quote that is "pulled" from the article and set in larger type on the page right in the middle of visually boring text. The idea is to draw the reader into the article because he read the shocking quote and wants to find out more. You can either just enlarge the type and place it between two rules or in a box, or you can really dress it up by designing it, which will make the quotes act like illustrations.

Repetition: One of the design rules or principles of design. Repeating designs, type or illustrations on a page to make a creative layout. Repetition creates visual *rhythm, movement,* and *unity.* But it can also be hypnotic and boring if you don't use repetition with variation.

Repetition With Variation: Repeating design elements endlessly in the same exact way tends to become boring or even hypnotic if overdone. But if you see slight variations among the elements that are repeating, then your eyes take notice right away. This design rule can also be used to create a sense of movement in your layout.

Resolution: The number of pixels (lighted dots) on a computer screen. The more pixels per inch, the higher the resolution. Ex. 800 x 600. The measure of resolution is usually expressed as "dpi" (dots per inch).

RGB Color: The type of color used on your computer monitor. This color structure is based on the three primary colors of Red, Green and Blue and they are composed of light being mixed and emitted from within your computer monitor to create 256, thousands, or millions of colors.

Rhythm: One of the design rules or principles of design. Normally, rhythm is associated with music. But rhythm can be visual also. By repeating lines, or other design objects an arresting visual rhythm can be created. The illusion of motion can also be created with the aid of a "fast" visual rhythm.

Just as the rhythm of the music fits the action in a movie, likewise the visual rhythm in your layout fits the subject of your layout.

Rows: A horizontal linear arrangement used in laying out type, photos, a chart or a diagram.

Roy G. Biv: A pneumonic device for remembering the order of colors in the rainbow: Red, Orange, Yellow, Green, Blue, Indigo (Blue-Violet), Violet.

Rule: A perfectly straight line. Rules can vary in thickness and are used as design elements to separate type or to create borders on a page.

Runaround: When a graphic object is placed in the middle of a block of text, the text is forced to flow around the graphic object so that the text can still be easily read. This new text flow changes the shape of the column of type.

Sans Serif: The strokes of these letters are all the same thickness and they come without (or "sans" in French) any extra cross strokes (serifs) at the end of the main strokes.

Scanning: Converting any existing art to a digital image that can be edited or stored.

Scope of work: A document that is written for the person doing the work, usually included with the contract for the work to be done. Includes a complete list of criteria the project must meet. It may include a design brief, specification, or storyboard.

Script: A way of handwriting where all the letter forms are connected in a seemingly unending pen stroke. This Script or handwriting style was initially done with "quills" or large feathers plucked from birds such as geese and then dipped into bottles of ink. If you split the end of the quill, then it holds ink better and if you vary the pressure you place on it, you can get elegant thicks and thins to your letters. Nowadays this is a category of type where the fonts mimic this old-style handwriting.

Search engine: A database of URLs on the web that can be searched by key word or key phrase.

Security: In reference to computers, security can be related to computer access, data access, or data integrity. This can include user names, passwords, and biometric recognition, and is used to limit or permit access to computers, drives, servers, directories, or specific files.

Serif: Instead of abruptly ending, the vertical strokes of type smoothly curve or transition into horizontal cross strokes or "feet." This makes the letter look more pleasing, and allows the human eye to easily transition from one letter to the next.

Shape: One of the tools or elements of design. There are geometric shapes like rectangles, circles, hexagons, etc. Then there are freeform shapes and abstract shapes. You can use shapes in layout design and logo design to create panels, boxes and shapes that look like people, animals, and objects.

Sidebar: An interesting very short mini-article, accompanying a larger article. Sidebars are filled with tips or other practical information, and are usually related to the main articles they appear with but have a slightly different focus. They do the same thing as a pull quote or photo by adding interest to the layout of the page.

Silhouetted Photo: A photo of an object, person or etc. with the background removed. Also known as an Outlined Photo.

Size: One of the design tools or elements of design. How big or small something is in relation to other elements on the page. Size determines importance, evokes a sense of depth, and can be used to create unity.

Sketchy: A style of illustration that's rough and loose. It gives the appearance that it's been done quickly or without much effort.

Slogan: A catchy phrase used in advertising and promotion that becomes associated with a product or service's identity.

Small Caps: A method of using

all caps but making the words look like they were set in Upper and Lower Case because some of the caps are smaller than the initial caps.

Space: One of the design tools or elements of design. The space around and between objects and type is just as tangible as the objects and type themselves. The most obvious use of space is the proximity of things to each other on a page. Space can make a layout easier on the eyes.

Spread: Two pages in a book, magazine or newspaper which face each other when the publication is opened. A two-page spread is also known as a "double truck."

Still Life: A picture whose subject is inanimate objects such as flowers, fruit, or various things on a table or desk.

Stipple: A technique of shading a drawing or painting using dots. The closer the dots are, the darker the value. The further apart the dots are, the lighter the value. Also known as Pontilism or Pointillism.

Storyboard: This is a method used to determine the screens that will make up a web site or any computer application. It would be similar to the storyboards used when sequencing movies and commercials.

Subhead: Subtitles set in bold type which break the text into smaller sections for easier reading. A page with subheads is more reader-friendly than a page of solid body copy, because you don't feel like you have to read the entire page at once – just a small section.

Symbol Type: Graphic Objects that have been turned into font format. Symbol type is usually specialized Greek letters. Symbol type falls into the same category of type as Clip Art fonts.

Symmetry: In a layout or composition, a type of balance where all

the elements are centered or have a mirror image effect with the vertical axis at the center. Opposite of asymmetrical balance where everything is off-centered.

Technical Illustration: A very precise form of illustration with mechanical and scientific objects, tools, machinery, cars, trucks, appliances, etc. used as subjects.

Text: See Body Text.

Text Flow: The direction in which body text reads on a page. The direction of flow can go down one column then up to the top of the next. Or it can flow around a graphic object that's in the middle of the page.

Texture: One of the design tools or elements of design. The basis of texture begins with the sense of touch. There is a visual sense to textures, because of a pattern of light and dark (values) unique to each texture.

Three Dimensions: In the real world the three dimensions are width, height and depth. On paper there are only two dimensions: width and height. So the only way to create three dimensions on paper is by illusion. Type can be made more exciting by making it appear three dimensional.

Tight: A style of illustration that's precise, detailed and looks like it's been done with straight edges or computers and has taken a long time to do.

Trapping: When two areas of color touch each other, their edges have to slightly overlap (overprint) to create the illusion that they perfectly align (register) with each other. If their edges don't slightly overlap, then, because of the variation in the movement of each piece of paper through the press, there will be a tiny white gap between one area of color and another on some of the printed pieces.

Typeface: A unique design for the letters of the alphabet. Typographers have designed hundreds of typefaces, known as fonts, which are used for both body text and headline text by typists and graphic designers to create professional typesetting.

Underlines: A line underneath a word or group of words used to draw attention to those words.

Unity: One of the design rules or principles of design. All the elements of a layout look like they belong together when there is unity.

Upper Case: Capital letters.

Up-time: The time that any system is running, active, and ready for use.

URL: Universal Resource Locator. The URL is part of the addressing system used on the web, and also on any networked computer. It contains information about the server, method of access, and the path to specific data. URL's can be used to access data from any connected server or disk. A sample URL: http://www.sixbranches.com.htm. See IP.

Value: One of the design tools or elements of design. Value has to do with a black and white scale that ranges from solid black to solid white. The steps in between are different shades of gray going from dark gray to light gray. There are usually about 10 steps in a value scale or grayscale. This grayscale is a standard by which you can measure the lightness or darkness of type or graphic objects on a page.

Vector Graphics: Made up of objects that are represented by vectors, lines with direction and magnitude, arcs, text, etc. Used in CAD and other drawing programs. The color, size, and direction of each element may be controlled by tiny electronic points called handles to control or modify the vectors of elements in some applications.

Vertical: Anything, such as a line, plane or object that is at right angles to the horizon. Also movement of anything can be considered vertical if it moves from top to bottom or bottom to top, which is considered at right angles to the horizon.

Virus: Any program, script, or other computer code that is loaded automatically onto your computer without your knowledge and runs automatically. Viruses can replicate themselves and attach themselves to other files. Worms are viruses that replicate, but do not attach themselves to other files.

Volume Number: A number used to designate each successive year of a magazine or newsletter. For example, if you have a monthly magazine that started in January, it's in its second year of publication and this month is May, it would be known as Volume 2, Issue 5.

Wallpaper Technique: Wallpaper and wrapping paper use the same technique of repeating images, designs or type to create textured backgrounds. The rhythm of lights and darks establishes a pattern with no real focal point that helps shade part of your layout.

Web Hosting: A web host is a company that offers servers or virtual servers to the public for the sole purpose of having your site accessed by others. This can be for public access, private access, web related, or FTP.

Weight: A characteristic of type describing whether it is thin or thick in varying degrees. Type can be Light, Regular (also known as Medium), Bold, Demi Bold, Black and even Ultra Black.

White Space: The space around and between graphic objects and type on a page or in an ad. A professional layout always manages to work in white space to enhance the feeling of openness and readability, thereby improving the sense of design. White space does not just exist for the sole purpose of being filled with type or graphic objects. It is just as tangible a design element as the objects and type themselves – just as "0" (zero) is just as viable a number as 1, 2, 3 or etc.

WYSIWYG: What You See Is What You Get. The way you see it on the screen or monitor is the way it is going to print.

x height: The vertical section of a letter that does not include ascenders or descenders. For example, in the word "freight" the "r," "e," and "i" represent the "x" height of letters and the "f," "h," and "t" represent letters with ascenders that rise above the "x" height of the letter. The "g" represents a letter with a descender dropping below the "x" height of the letter.

RESOURCES

Print Resources:

Communication Arts Magazine, 110 Constitution Drive, Menlo Park, CA 94025

Creative Visual Thinking, How To Think Up Ideas Fast, by Morton Garchik, 1982, Art Direction Book Company

Designing and Writing Online Documentation, by William K. Horton

Graphic Design Made Difficult, by Bob Gill, 1992, Van Nostrand Reinhold

Graphic Idea Notebook, Inventive Techniques For Designing Printed Pages, by Jan V. White, 1980, Watson-Guptill Publications

Jakob Nielsen's 10 usability heuristics (search the web for this phrase)

Making a Good Layout, by Lori Siebert & Lisa Ballard, 1992, North Light Books

Managing Software Requirements, A Unified Approach, by Dean Leffingwell & Don Widrig

Newsletter Sourcebook, by Mark Beach, 1993, North Light Books

The Non-Designer's Design Book, Design and Typographic Principles for the Visual Novice, by Robin Williams, 1994, Peachpit Press

Print Magazine, America's Graphic Design Magazine, Editorial Offices, 116 East 27th Street, 6th Floor, New York, NY 10016. Circulation Dept., 700 E. State St. Iola, WI 54945-9984.

Standards for Online Communication, by Joann T. Hackos

Type Rules, The Designer's Guide to Professional Typography, by Ilene Strizver, 2001, North Light Books

A Typographic Workbook, by Kate Clair, 1999, John Wiley & Sons, Inc.

Internet Resources:

www/commarts.com (*Communication Arts Magazine* website)

www.howdesign.com (*How Magazine* website)

www.printmag.com (*Print Magazine, America's Graphic Design Magazine* website)

www.pcwebopaedia.com

www.techweb.com

www.loc.gov/copyright/

http://thorplus.lib.purdue.edu/reference/dict.html